For Raquel–I'm literally Mexican because of you–TB

For Diamela–te quiero abuelita–MJ

PENGUIN WORKSHOP
An Imprint of Penguin Random House LLC, New York

Penguin supports copyright. Copyright fuels creativity, encourages diverse voices, promotes free speech, and creates a vibrant culture. Thank you for buying an authorized edition of this book and for complying with copyright laws by not reproducing, scanning, or distributing any part of it in any form without permission. You are supporting writers and allowing Penguin to continue to publish books for every reader.

The publisher does not have any control over and does not assume any responsibility for author or third-party websites or their content.

Copyright © 2021 by Penguin Random House LLC. All rights reserved.
Published by Penguin Workshop, an imprint of Penguin Random House LLC, New York.
PENGUIN and PENGUIN WORKSHOP are trademarks of Penguin Books Ltd.
WHO HQ & Design is a registered trademark of Penguin Random House LLC.
Manufactured in China.

Visit us online at www.penguinrandomhouse.com.

Library of Congress Cataloging-in-Publication Data is available upon request.

ISBN 9780593224496 (pbk)   10 9 8 7 6 5 4 3 2 1 HH
ISBN 9780593224502 (hc)   10 9 8 7 6 5 4 3 2 1 HH

Lettering by Comicraft
Book design by Jay Emmanuel

This is a work of nonfiction. All of the events that unfold in the narrative are rooted in historical fact. Some dialogue and characters have been fictionalized in order to illustrate or teach a historical point.

For more information about your favorite historical figures, places, and events, please visit www.whohq.com.

A WHO HQ GRAPHIC NOVEL

Who Was the Voice of the People?

CESAR CHAVEZ

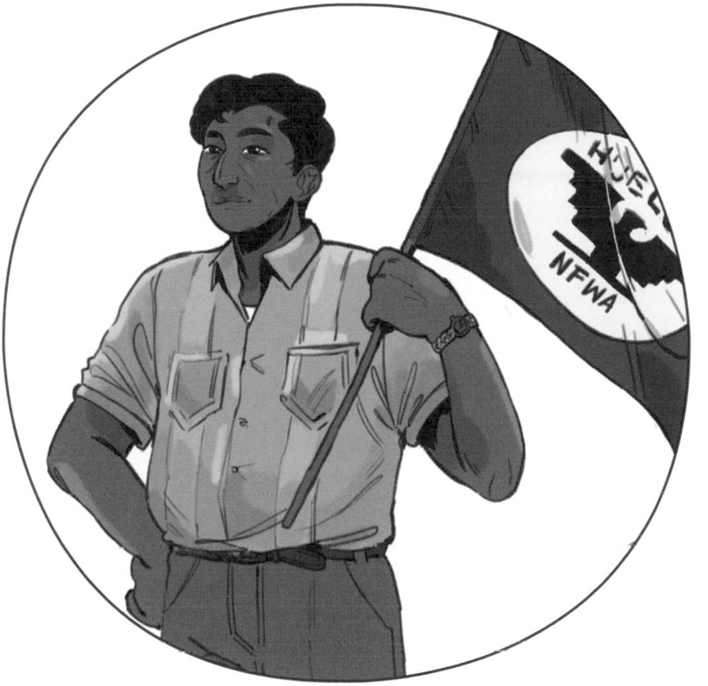
NFWA

by Terry Blas
illustrated by Mar Julia

Penguin Workshop

Introduction

Cesar Chavez was born on March 31, 1927, just outside Yuma, Arizona. His family lived in the Sonoran Desert on a ranch, which was bought by his grandparents, Mama Tella and Papa Chayo. They emigrated from Mexico to the United States in 1898. Papa Chayo died before Cesar was born, and Cesar spent his early childhood living with Mama Tella, his parents, Librado and Juana, and his siblings, Richard, Librado, Vicki, and Rita. Cesar's grandmother lived in the main adobe house, while Cesar's family lived in a small cottage on the main ranch. Together, the family worked on tending the land: feeding the animals, collecting eggs, and hauling water to the house.

Cesar didn't like school because the other kids made fun of the color of his skin. The teacher would punish him for speaking Spanish by hitting him on the knuckles with a ruler. He wanted to go outside and kick off his shoes. In class, he wanted to sit with his sister, but the teacher wouldn't allow it because boys were supposed to sit together, separate from the girls.

When Cesar was twelve, his family lost their ranch because of the Great Depression. They had to relocate to California, where there was more work in the fields of the farms. Cesar began working in the fields with his father and noticed what horrible conditions many had to suffer through. A lot of farmworkers worked long hours in the sun with very little pay, no bathrooms, and no meal breaks.

Cesar was heavily influenced by his mother, who ran the household and didn't condone any fighting among her children. But at a young age, Cesar became interested in the teachings of Mahatma Gandhi, a political leader who used nonviolent protest to lead India to independence from Britain. Gandhi's teachings greatly inspired Cesar—he also wanted to create change for farmworkers and his community in a peaceful way.

As he continued to witness the injustices done to farmworkers of many different races and ages, he decided to create a union—a group organized to protect workers' rights. The group called itself the National Farm Workers Association (NFWA). This angered many farm owners and companies who sold fruit and vegetables, especially grapes. One such company was Schenley Industries, which owned a few wineries and vineyards in California. Many migrant farmworkers labored at these vineyards under very poor conditions, struggling in the heat and unable to be part of a union.

In September 1965, the members of Cesar's union began to strike and started picketing at vineyards. They began to make signs and refused to work. But Cesar knew this wasn't enough. Something more had to be done.

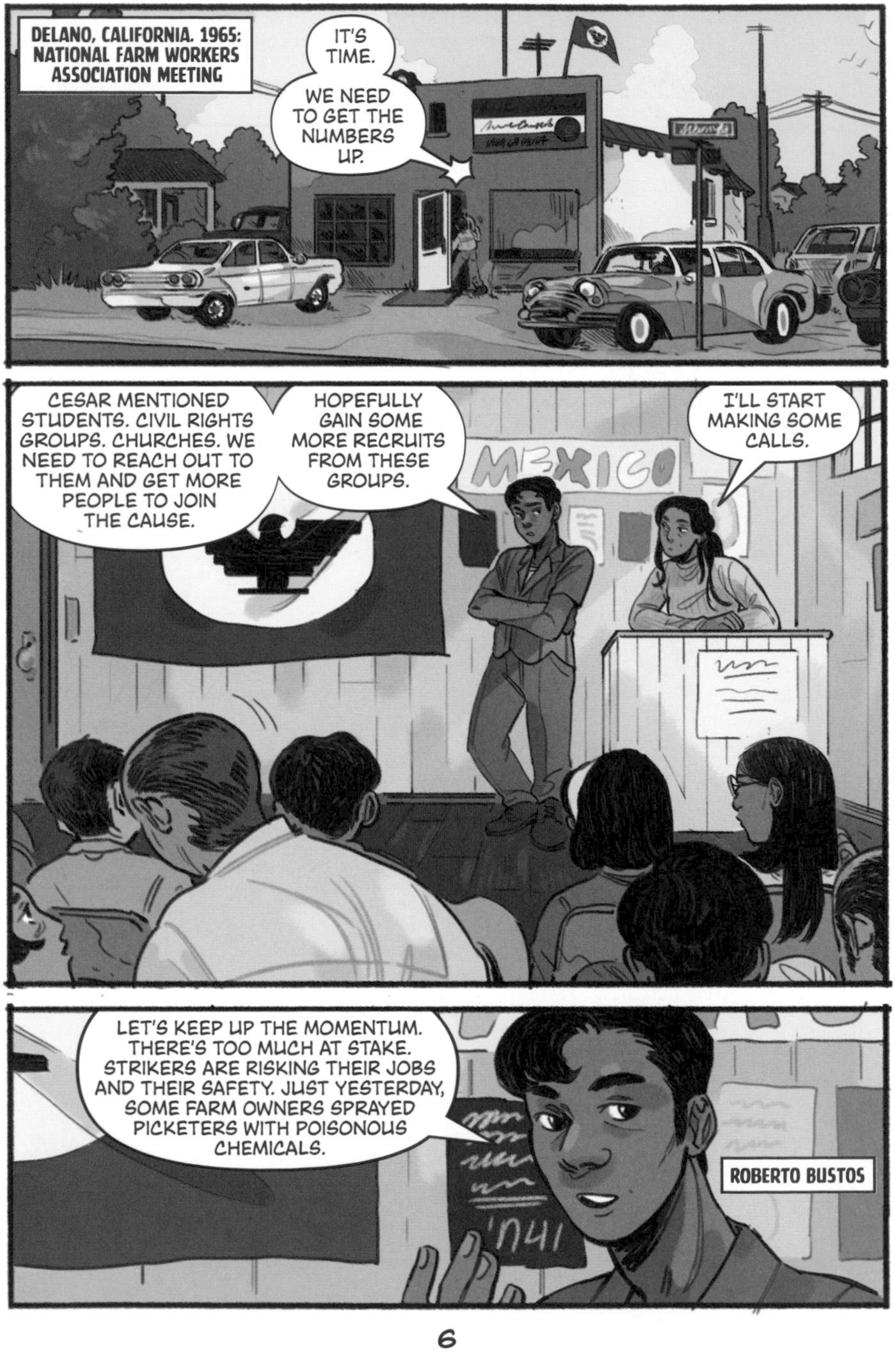
DELANO, CALIFORNIA. 1965: NATIONAL FARM WORKERS ASSOCIATION MEETING
IT'S TIME.
WE NEED TO GET THE NUMBERS UP.
CESAR MENTIONED STUDENTS. CIVIL RIGHTS GROUPS. CHURCHES. WE NEED TO REACH OUT TO THEM AND GET MORE PEOPLE TO JOIN THE CAUSE.
HOPEFULLY GAIN SOME MORE RECRUITS FROM THESE GROUPS.
MEXICO
I'LL START MAKING SOME CALLS.
LET'S KEEP UP THE MOMENTUM. THERE'S TOO MUCH AT STAKE. STRIKERS ARE RISKING THEIR JOBS AND THEIR SAFETY. JUST YESTERDAY, SOME FARM OWNERS SPRAYED PICKETERS WITH POISONOUS CHEMICALS.
ROBERTO BUSTOS

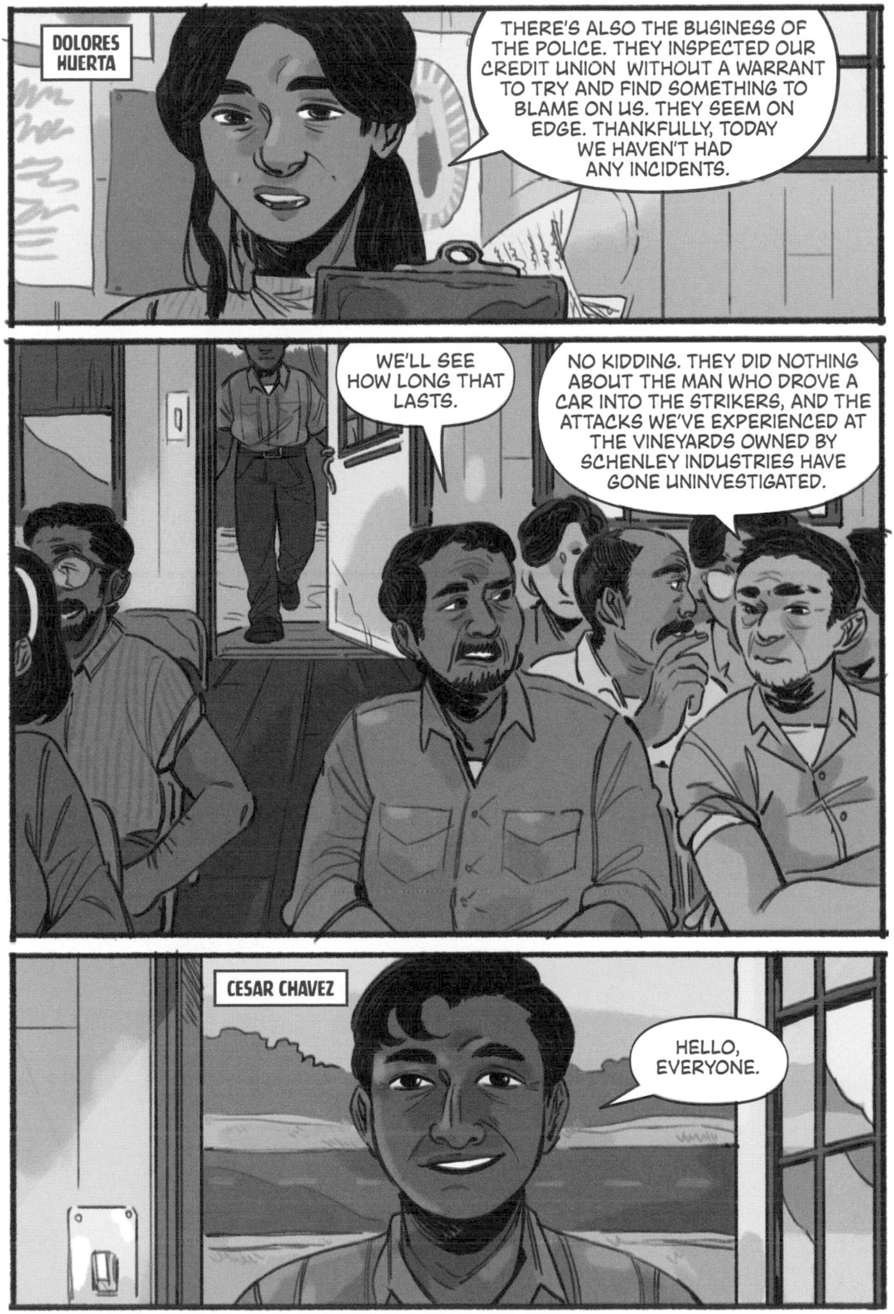
DOLORES HUERTA
THERE'S ALSO THE BUSINESS OF THE POLICE. THEY INSPECTED OUR CREDIT UNION WITHOUT A WARRANT TO TRY AND FIND SOMETHING TO BLAME ON US. THEY SEEM ON EDGE. THANKFULLY, TODAY WE HAVEN'T HAD ANY INCIDENTS.
WE'LL SEE HOW LONG THAT LASTS.
NO KIDDING. THEY DID NOTHING ABOUT THE MAN WHO DROVE A CAR INTO THE STRIKERS, AND THE ATTACKS WE'VE EXPERIENCED AT THE VINEYARDS OWNED BY SCHENLEY INDUSTRIES HAVE GONE UNINVESTIGATED.
CESAR CHAVEZ
HELLO, EVERYONE.

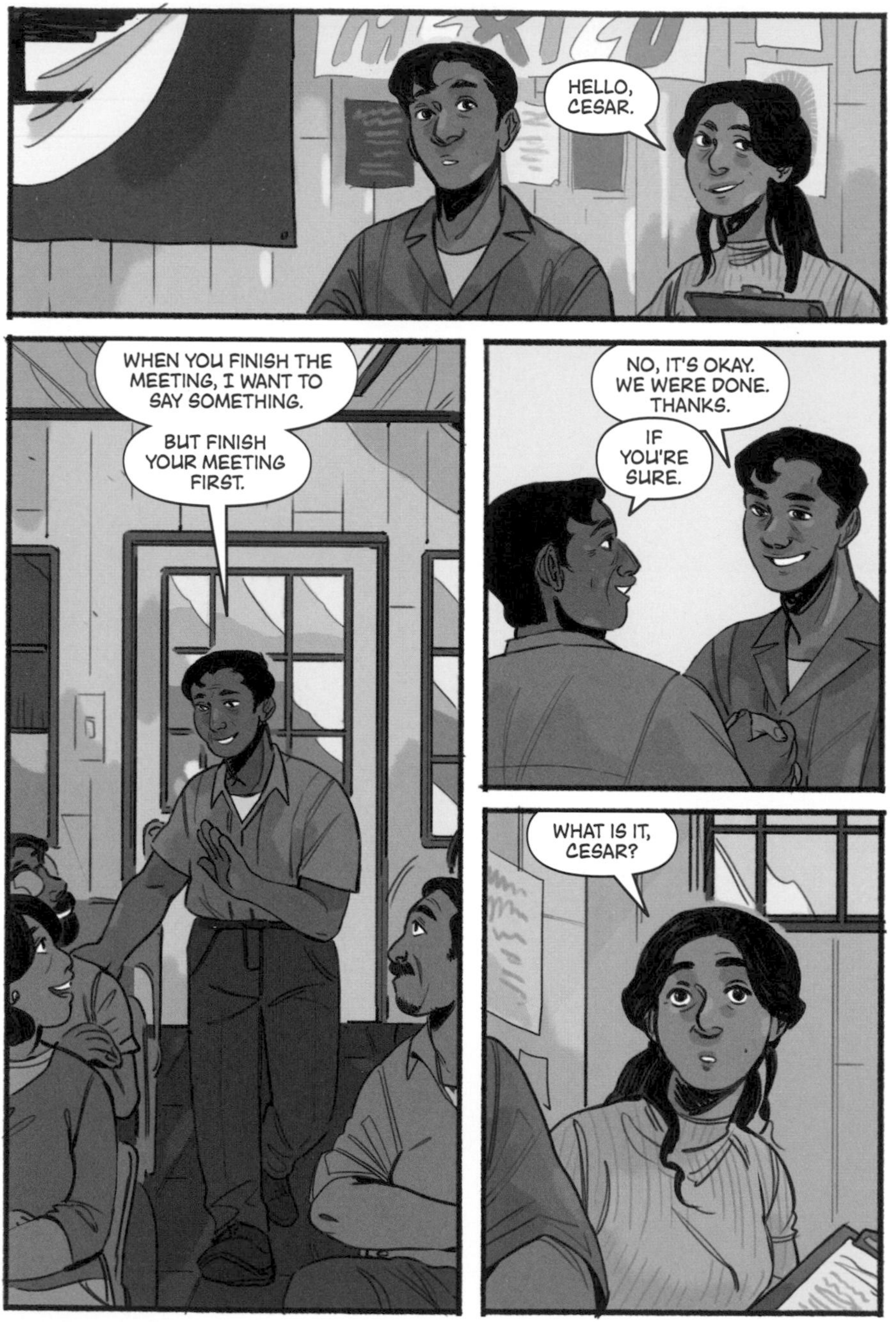
HELLO, CESAR.
WHEN YOU FINISH THE MEETING, I WANT TO SAY SOMETHING.
BUT FINISH YOUR MEETING FIRST.
NO, IT'S OKAY. WE WERE DONE. THANKS.
IF YOU'RE SURE.
WHAT IS IT, CESAR?

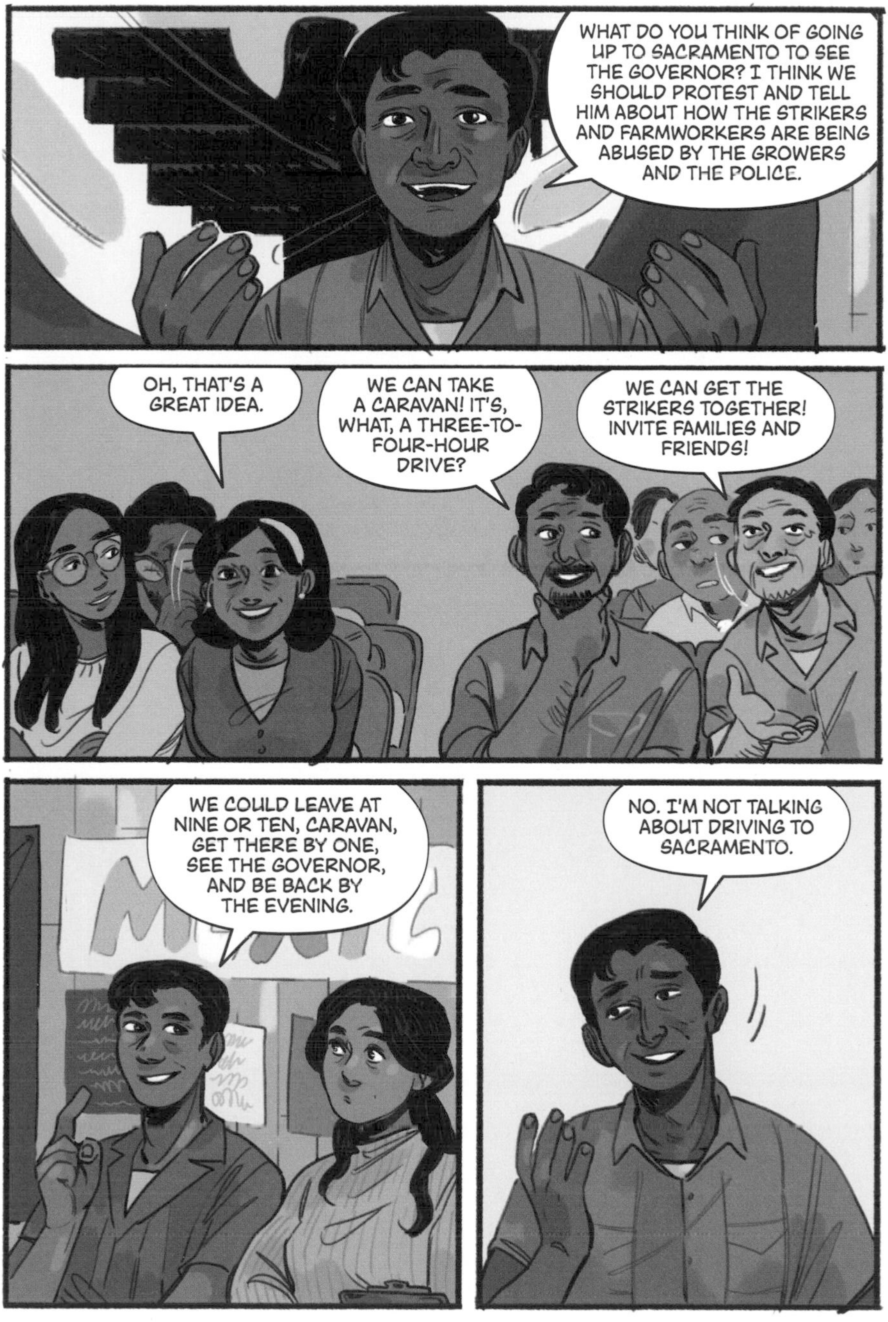
WHAT DO YOU THINK OF GOING UP TO SACRAMENTO TO SEE THE GOVERNOR? I THINK WE SHOULD PROTEST AND TELL HIM ABOUT HOW THE STRIKERS AND FARMWORKERS ARE BEING ABUSED BY THE GROWERS AND THE POLICE.
OH, THAT'S A GREAT IDEA.
WE CAN TAKE A CARAVAN! IT'S, WHAT, A THREE-TO-FOUR-HOUR DRIVE?
WE CAN GET THE STRIKERS TOGETHER! INVITE FAMILIES AND FRIENDS!
WE COULD LEAVE AT NINE OR TEN, CARAVAN, GET THERE BY ONE, SEE THE GOVERNOR, AND BE BACK BY THE EVENING.
NO. I'M NOT TALKING ABOUT DRIVING TO SACRAMENTO.

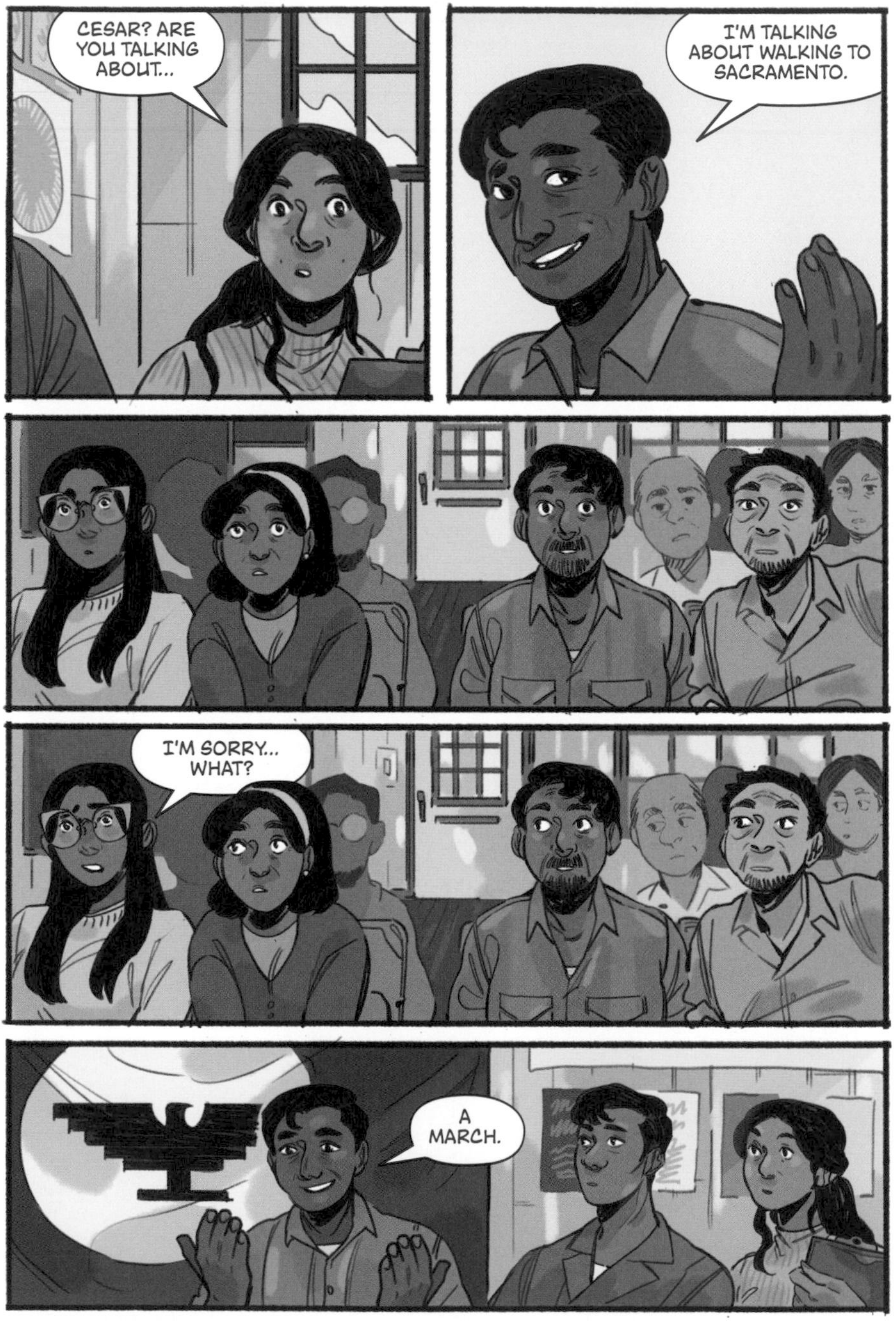
CESAR? ARE YOU TALKING ABOUT...
I'M TALKING ABOUT WALKING TO SACRAMENTO.
I'M SORRY... WHAT?
A MARCH.

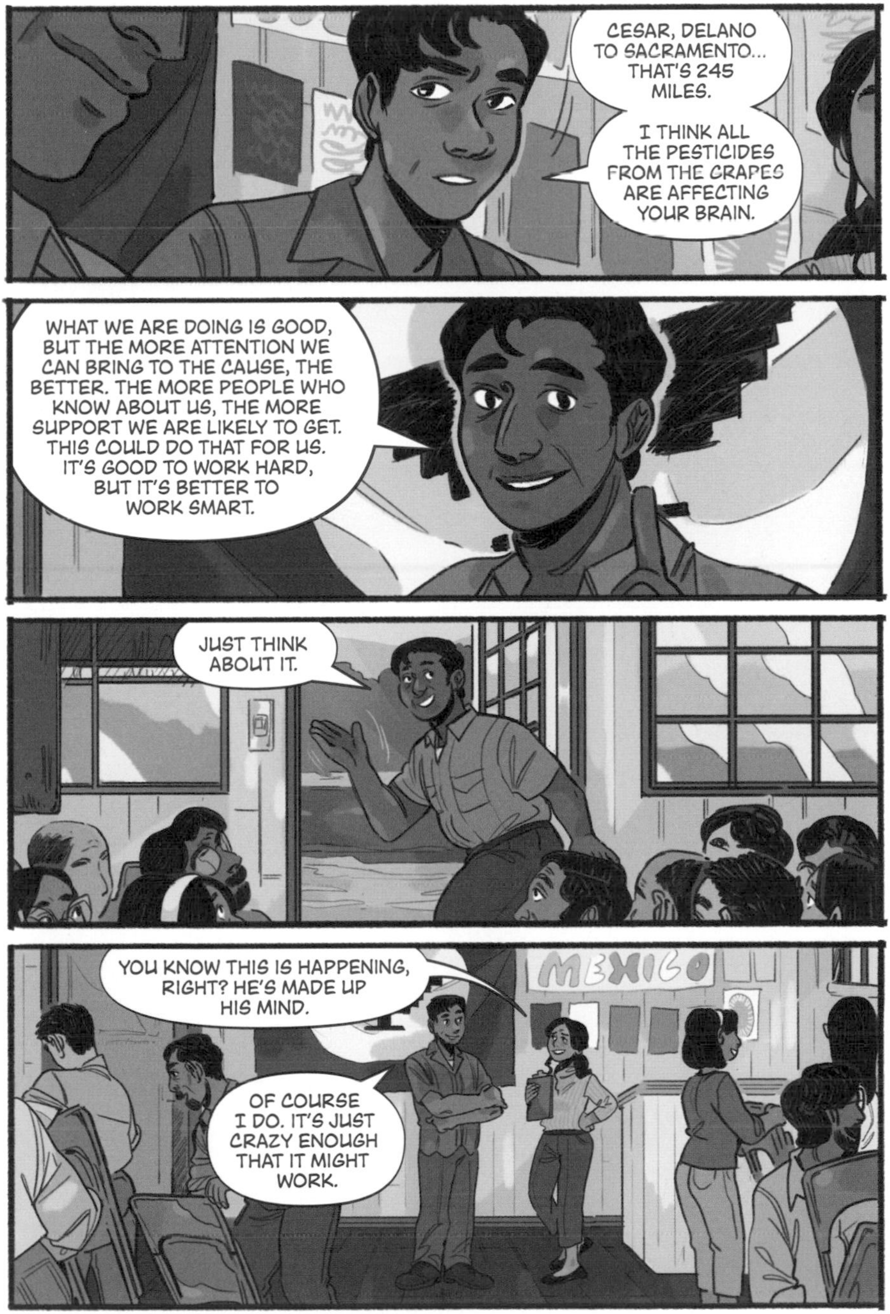
CESAR, DELANO TO SACRAMENTO... THAT'S 245 MILES.
I THINK ALL THE PESTICIDES FROM THE GRAPES ARE AFFECTING YOUR BRAIN.
WHAT WE ARE DOING IS GOOD, BUT THE MORE ATTENTION WE CAN BRING TO THE CAUSE, THE BETTER. THE MORE PEOPLE WHO KNOW ABOUT US, THE MORE SUPPORT WE ARE LIKELY TO GET. THIS COULD DO THAT FOR US. IT'S GOOD TO WORK HARD, BUT IT'S BETTER TO WORK SMART.
JUST THINK ABOUT IT.
YOU KNOW THIS IS HAPPENING, RIGHT? HE'S MADE UP HIS MIND.
MEXICO
OF COURSE I DO. IT'S JUST CRAZY ENOUGH THAT IT MIGHT WORK.

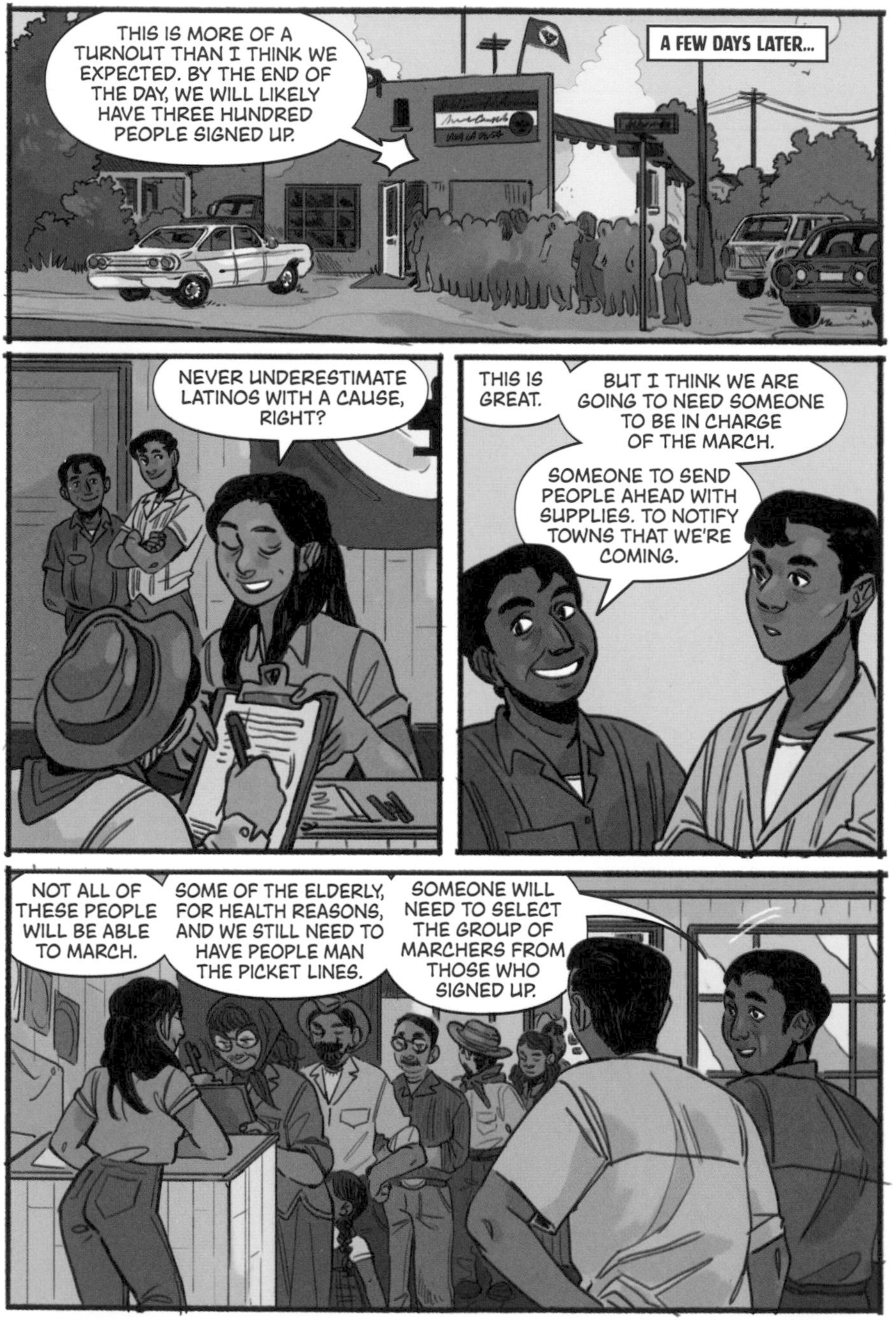
A FEW DAYS LATER...
THIS IS MORE OF A TURNOUT THAN I THINK WE EXPECTED. BY THE END OF THE DAY, WE WILL LIKELY HAVE THREE HUNDRED PEOPLE SIGNED UP.
NEVER UNDERESTIMATE LATINOS WITH A CAUSE, RIGHT?
THIS IS GREAT.
BUT I THINK WE ARE GOING TO NEED SOMEONE TO BE IN CHARGE OF THE MARCH.
SOMEONE TO SEND PEOPLE AHEAD WITH SUPPLIES. TO NOTIFY TOWNS THAT WE'RE COMING.
NOT ALL OF THESE PEOPLE WILL BE ABLE TO MARCH.
SOME OF THE ELDERLY, FOR HEALTH REASONS, AND WE STILL NEED TO HAVE PEOPLE MAN THE PICKET LINES.
SOMEONE WILL NEED TO SELECT THE GROUP OF MARCHERS FROM THOSE WHO SIGNED UP.

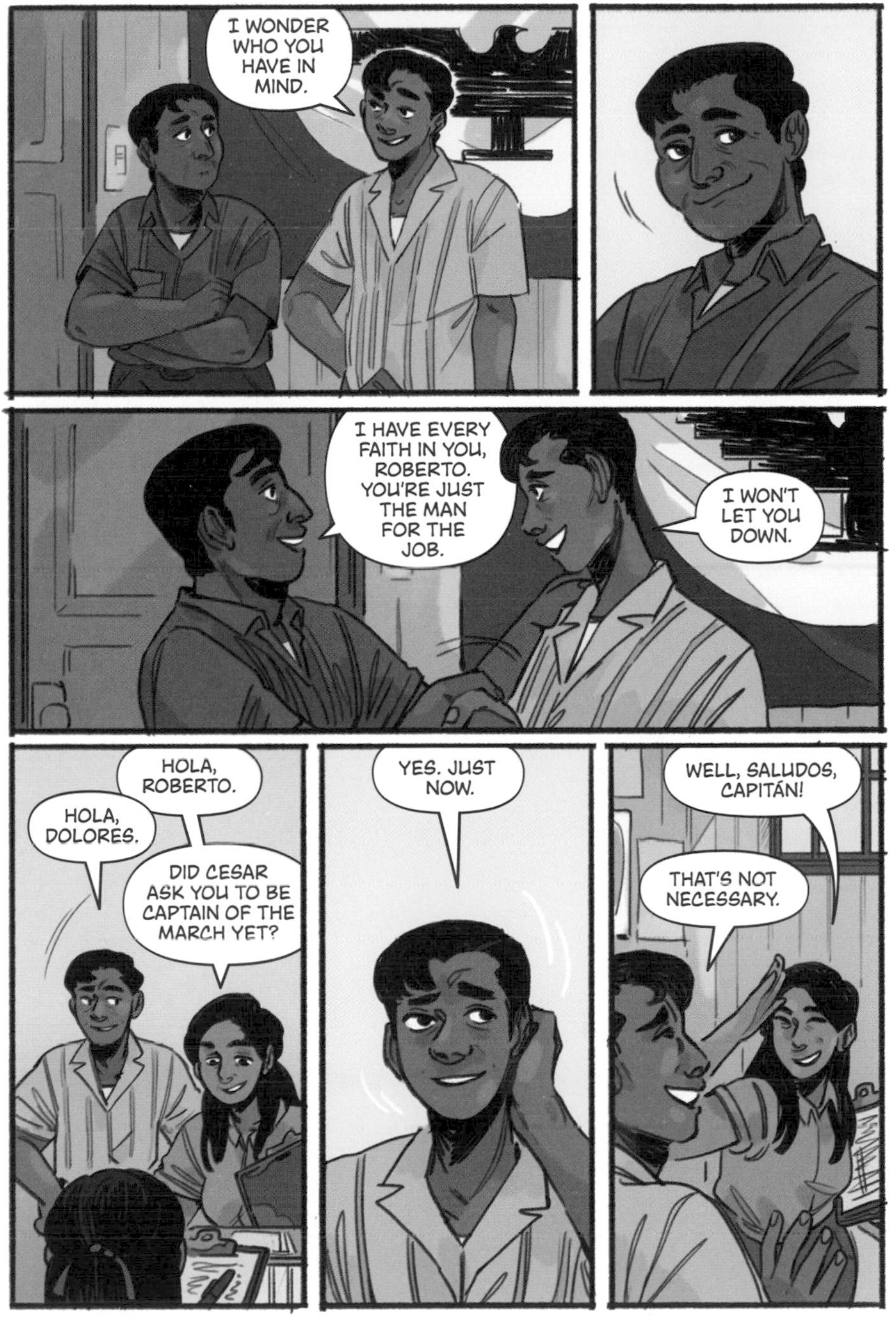
I WONDER WHO YOU HAVE IN MIND.
I HAVE EVERY FAITH IN YOU, ROBERTO. YOU'RE JUST THE MAN FOR THE JOB.
I WON'T LET YOU DOWN.
HOLA, DOLORES.
HOLA, ROBERTO.
DID CESAR ASK YOU TO BE CAPTAIN OF THE MARCH YET?
YES. JUST NOW.
WELL, SALUDOS, CAPITÁN!
THAT'S NOT NECESSARY.

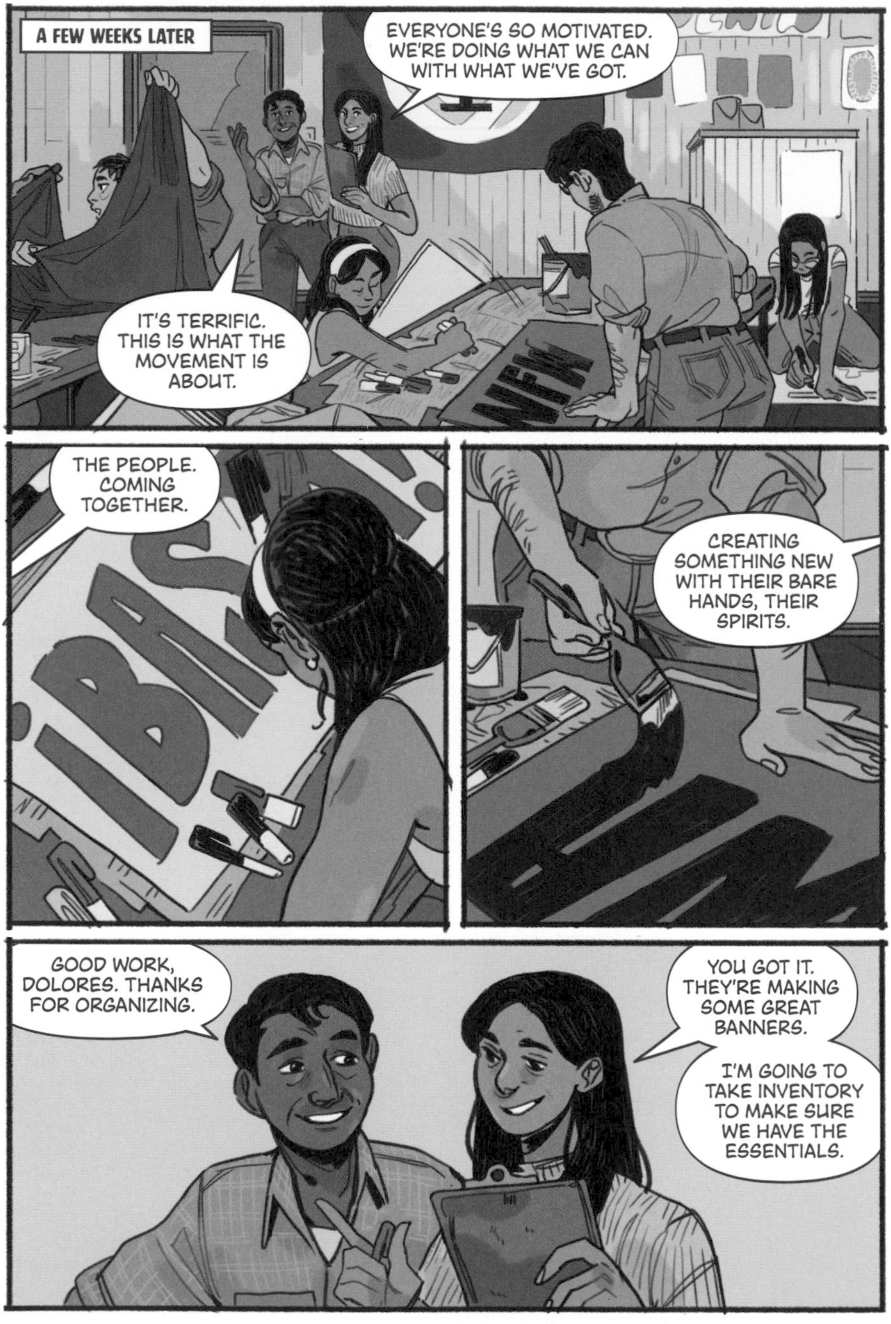
A FEW WEEKS LATER
EVERYONE'S SO MOTIVATED. WE'RE DOING WHAT WE CAN WITH WHAT WE'VE GOT.
IT'S TERRIFIC. THIS IS WHAT THE MOVEMENT IS ABOUT.
THE PEOPLE. COMING TOGETHER.
CREATING SOMETHING NEW WITH THEIR BARE HANDS, THEIR SPIRITS.
GOOD WORK, DOLORES. THANKS FOR ORGANIZING.
YOU GOT IT. THEY'RE MAKING SOME GREAT BANNERS.
I'M GOING TO TAKE INVENTORY TO MAKE SURE WE HAVE THE ESSENTIALS.

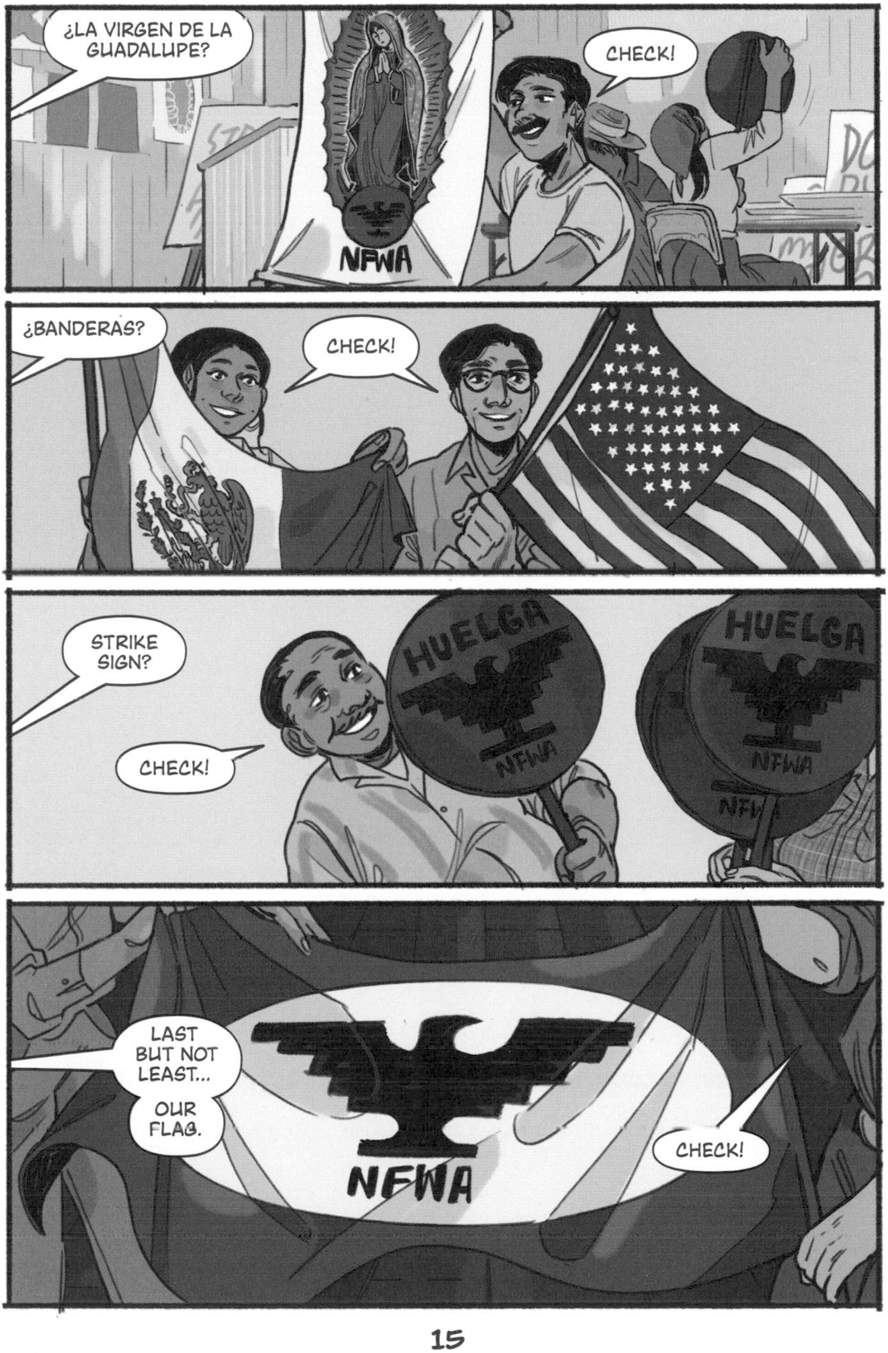
¿LA VIRGEN DE LA GUADALUPE?
NFWA
CHECK!
¿BANDERAS?
CHECK!
STRIKE SIGN?
HUELGA
NFWA
CHECK!
HUELGA
NFWA
NFWA
LAST BUT NOT LEAST...
OUR FLAG.
NFWA
CHECK!

NFWA Flag

In a theater in Fresno, California, at the first convention of the National Farm Workers Association, union members revealed their new flag. They displayed a red banner with a black eagle, its wings spread, over a white circle. Each color has a specific meaning. Black was meant to represent the hard life the farmworkers had to endure. Red was for the many sacrifices they would have to make, and white was for hope.

Cesar asked his brother Richard Chavez and his cousin Manuel Chavez to come up with a symbol that would be easy to recreate. Something anyone could make. They went with the eagle because of its importance to the Mexican flag and Mexican culture. The eagle was a bold, graphic shape—its wings mimicking the shape of Mesoamerican temples and pyramids.

"A symbol is an important thing," Cesar said. "That is why we chose an Aztec eagle. It gives pride. When people see it, they know it means dignity. To me, it looks like a strong, beautiful sign of hope."

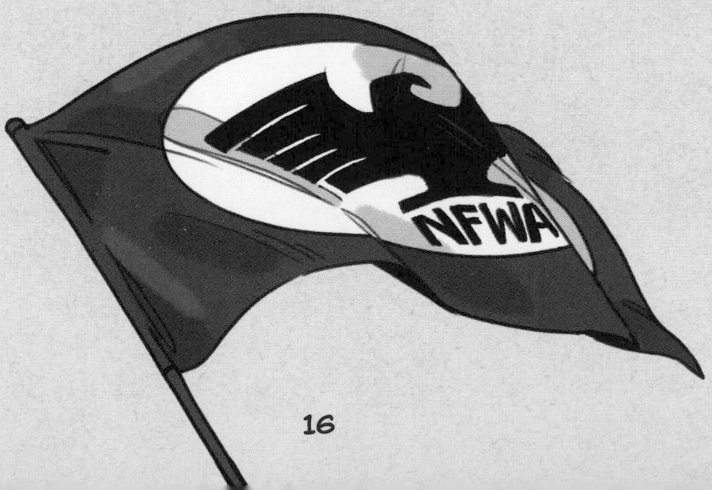
NFWA

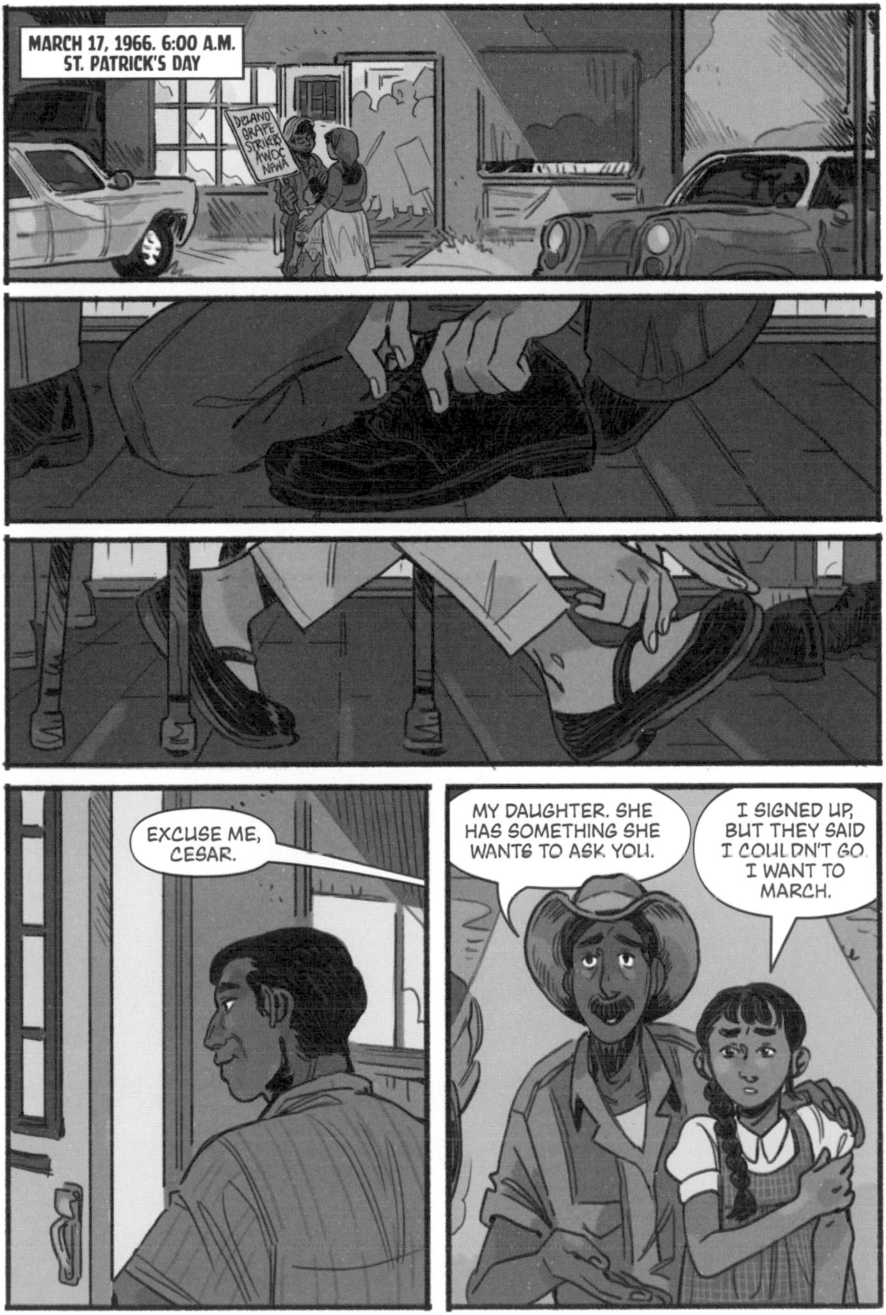
MARCH 17, 1966. 6:00 A.M.
ST. PATRICK'S DAY
DELANO GRAPE STRIKERS AWOC NFWA
EXCUSE ME, CESAR.
MY DAUGHTER. SHE HAS SOMETHING SHE WANTS TO ASK YOU.
I SIGNED UP, BUT THEY SAID I COULDN'T GO. I WANT TO MARCH.

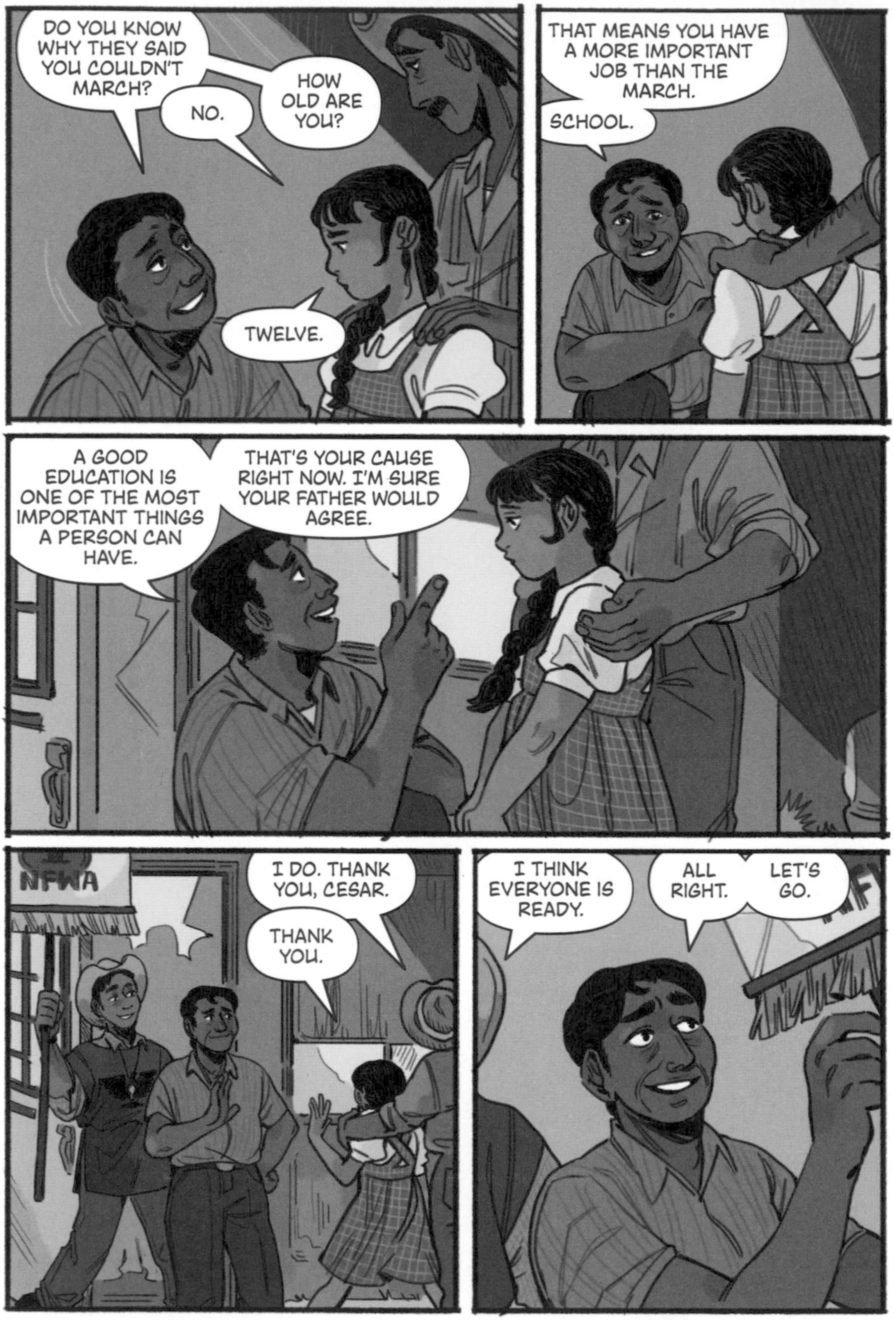
DO YOU KNOW WHY THEY SAID YOU COULDN'T MARCH?
NO.
HOW OLD ARE YOU?
TWELVE.
THAT MEANS YOU HAVE A MORE IMPORTANT JOB THAN THE MARCH.
SCHOOL.
A GOOD EDUCATION IS ONE OF THE MOST IMPORTANT THINGS A PERSON CAN HAVE.
THAT'S YOUR CAUSE RIGHT NOW. I'M SURE YOUR FATHER WOULD AGREE.
NFWA
I DO. THANK YOU, CESAR.
THANK YOU.
I THINK EVERYONE IS READY.
ALL RIGHT.
LET'S GO.

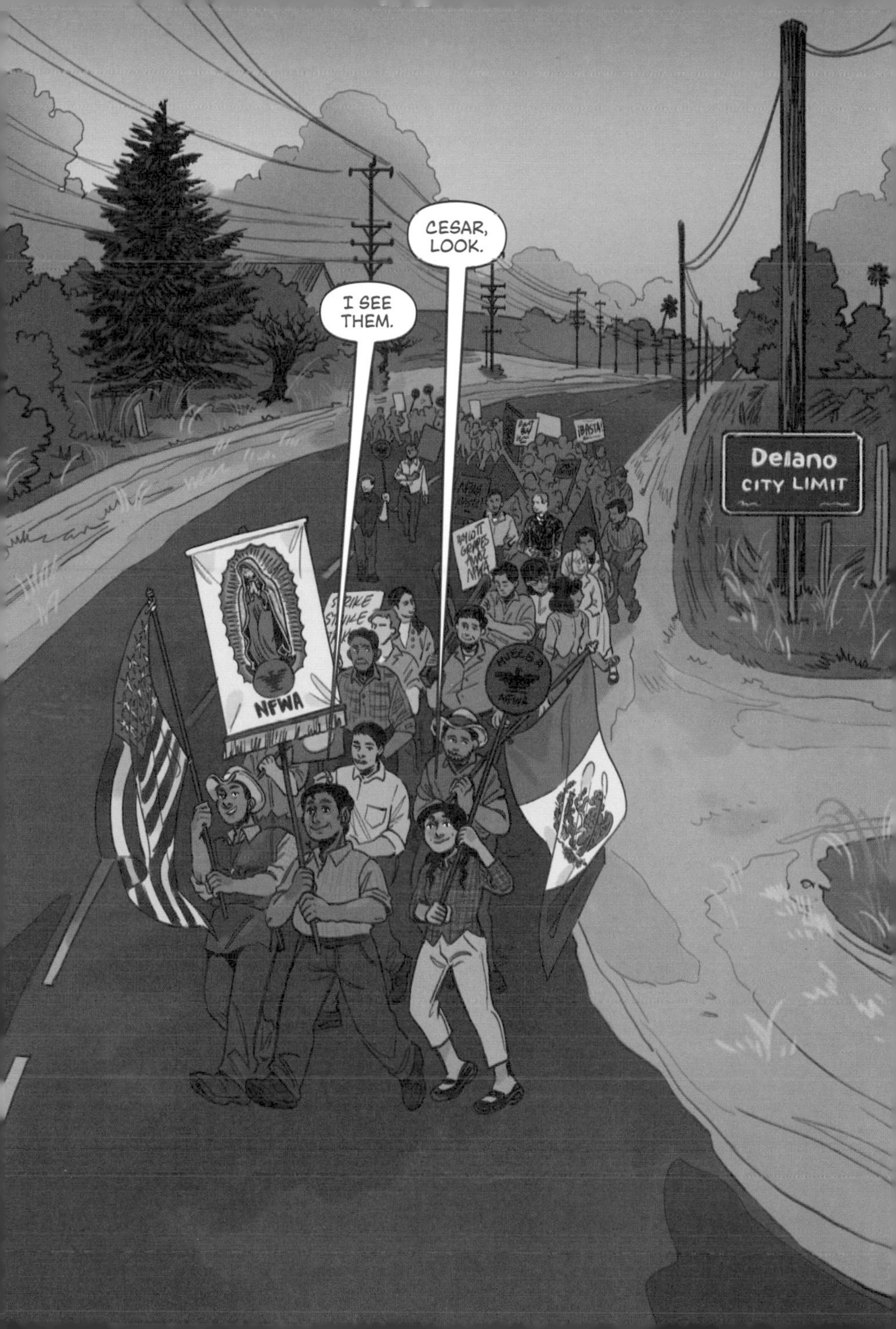
CESAR, LOOK.
I SEE THEM.
¡BASTA!
NFWA
Delano
CITY LIMIT

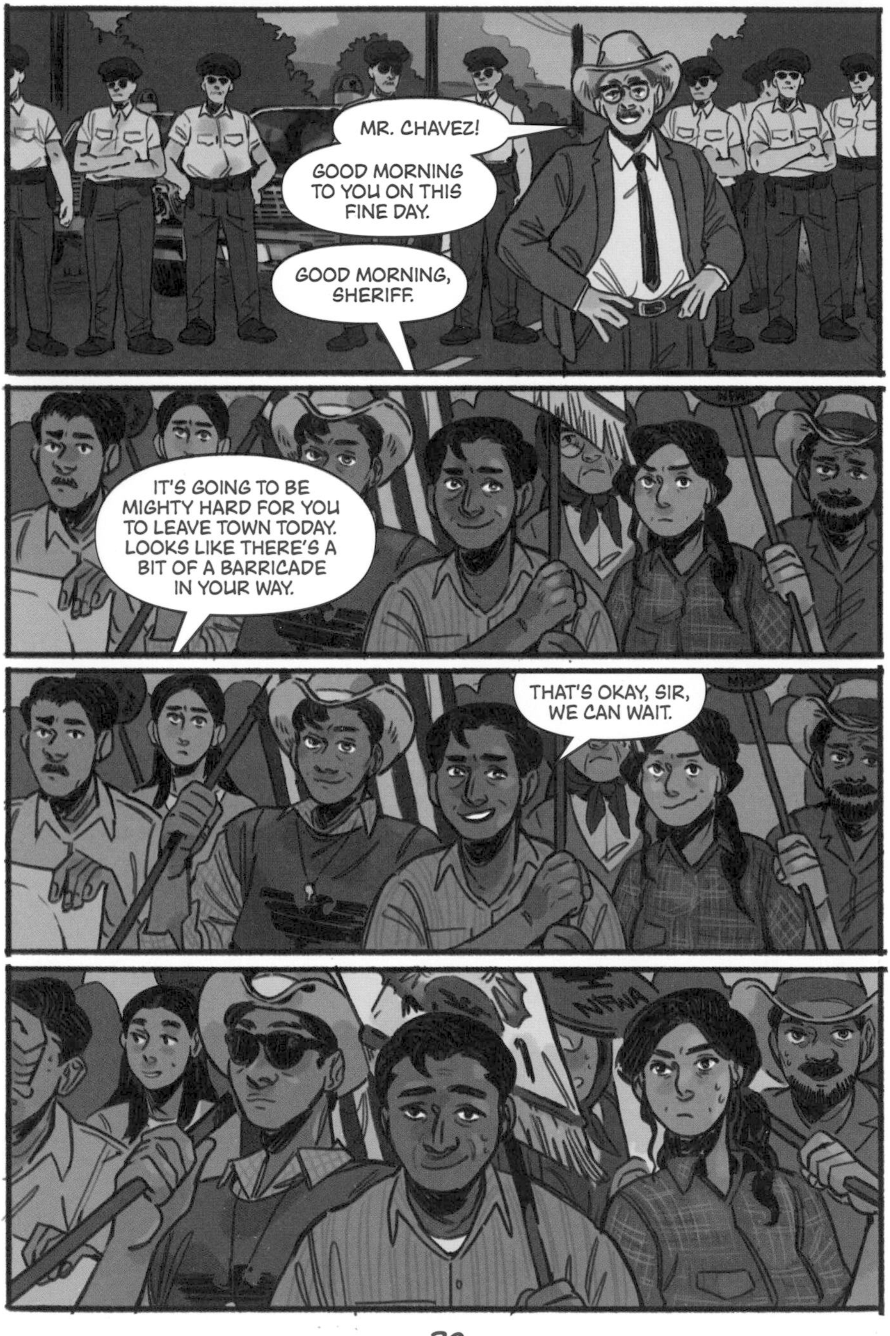
MR. CHAVEZ!
GOOD MORNING TO YOU ON THIS FINE DAY.
GOOD MORNING, SHERIFF.
IT'S GOING TO BE MIGHTY HARD FOR YOU TO LEAVE TOWN TODAY. LOOKS LIKE THERE'S A BIT OF A BARRICADE IN YOUR WAY.
THAT'S OKAY, SIR, WE CAN WAIT.

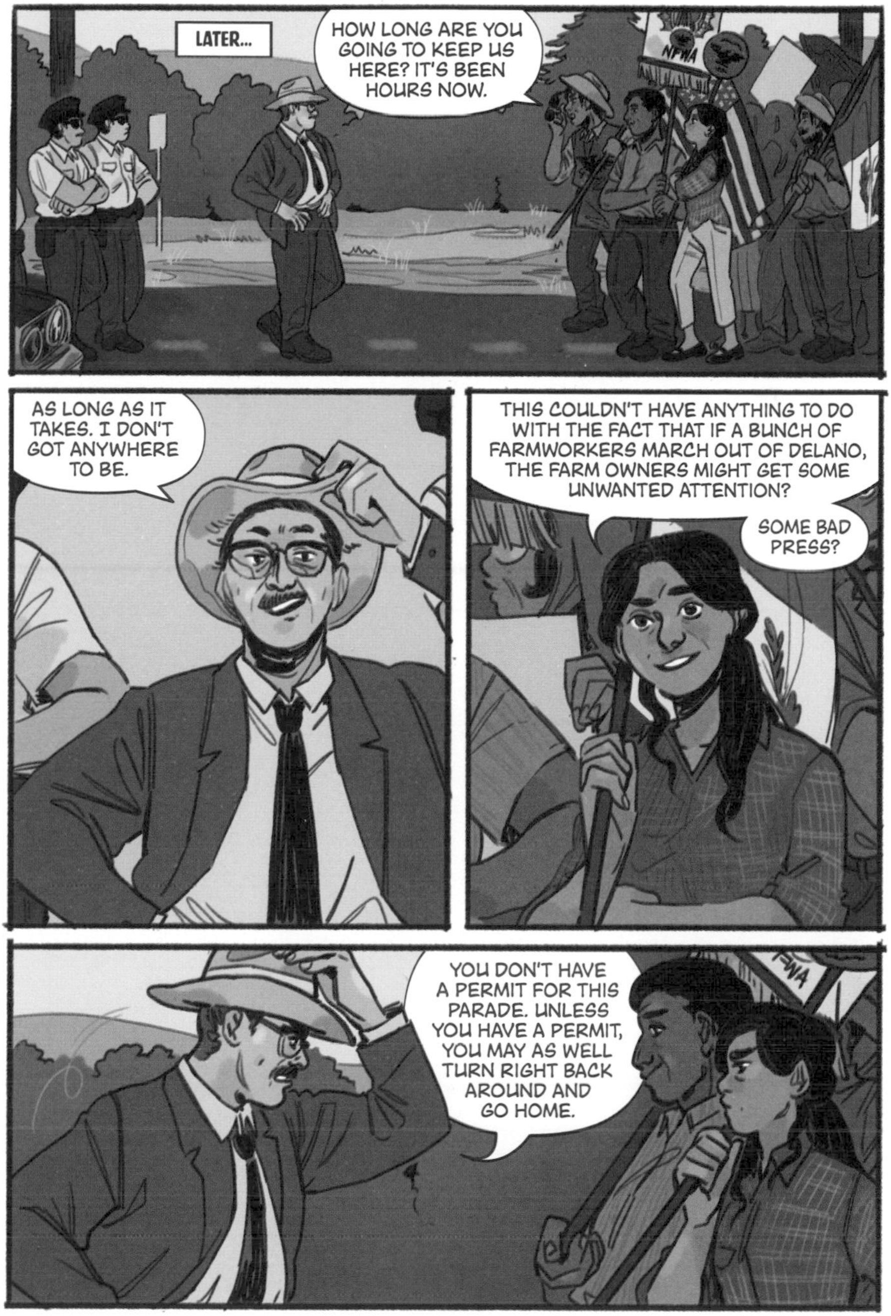
LATER...
HOW LONG ARE YOU GOING TO KEEP US HERE? IT'S BEEN HOURS NOW.
NFWA
AS LONG AS IT TAKES. I DON'T GOT ANYWHERE TO BE.
THIS COULDN'T HAVE ANYTHING TO DO WITH THE FACT THAT IF A BUNCH OF FARMWORKERS MARCH OUT OF DELANO, THE FARM OWNERS MIGHT GET SOME UNWANTED ATTENTION?
SOME BAD PRESS?
YOU DON'T HAVE A PERMIT FOR THIS PARADE. UNLESS YOU HAVE A PERMIT, YOU MAY AS WELL TURN RIGHT BACK AROUND AND GO HOME.

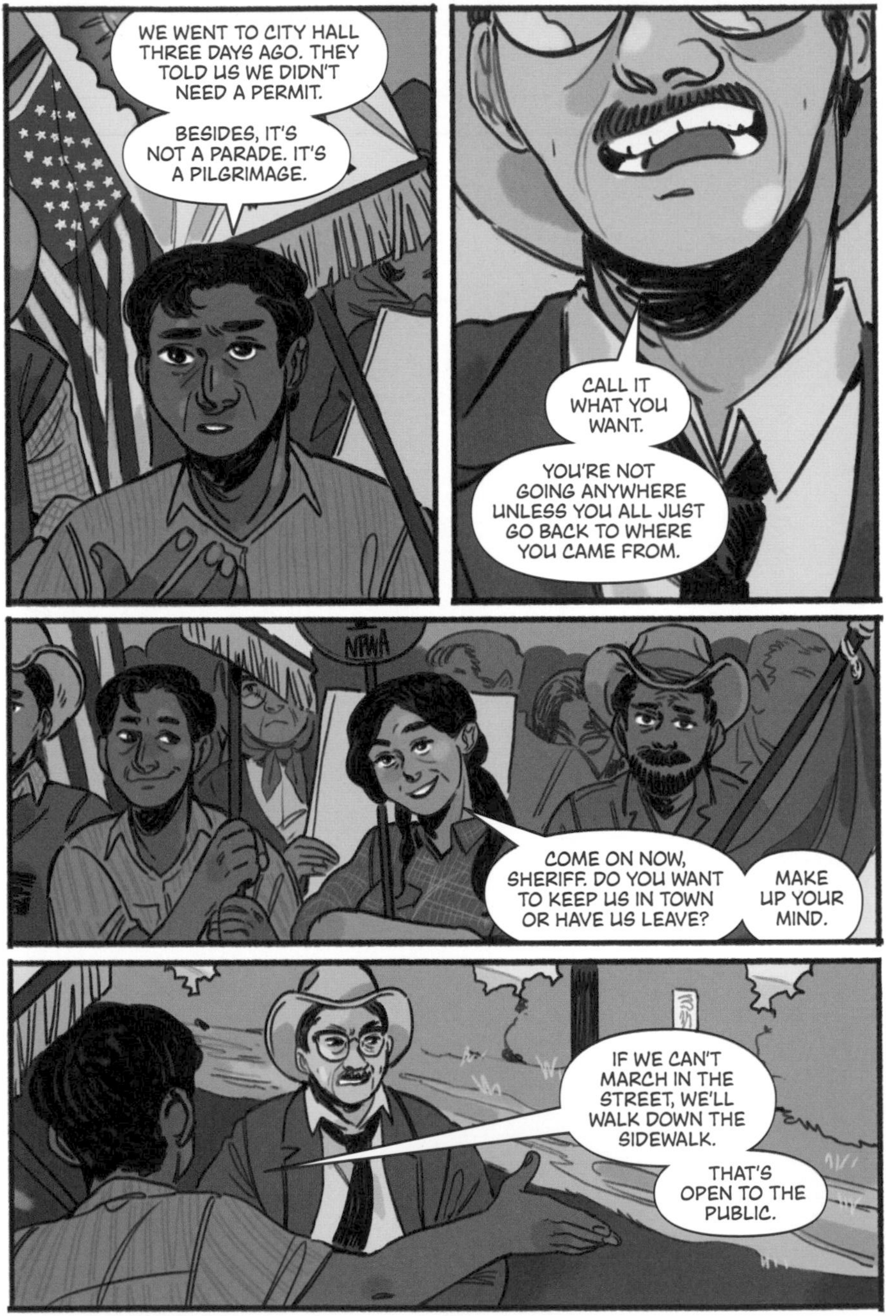
WE WENT TO CITY HALL THREE DAYS AGO. THEY TOLD US WE DIDN'T NEED A PERMIT.
BESIDES, IT'S NOT A PARADE. IT'S A PILGRIMAGE.
CALL IT WHAT YOU WANT.
YOU'RE NOT GOING ANYWHERE UNLESS YOU ALL JUST GO BACK TO WHERE YOU CAME FROM.
NFWA
COME ON NOW, SHERIFF. DO YOU WANT TO KEEP US IN TOWN OR HAVE US LEAVE?
MAKE UP YOUR MIND.
IF WE CAN'T MARCH IN THE STREET, WE'LL WALK DOWN THE SIDEWALK.
THAT'S OPEN TO THE PUBLIC.

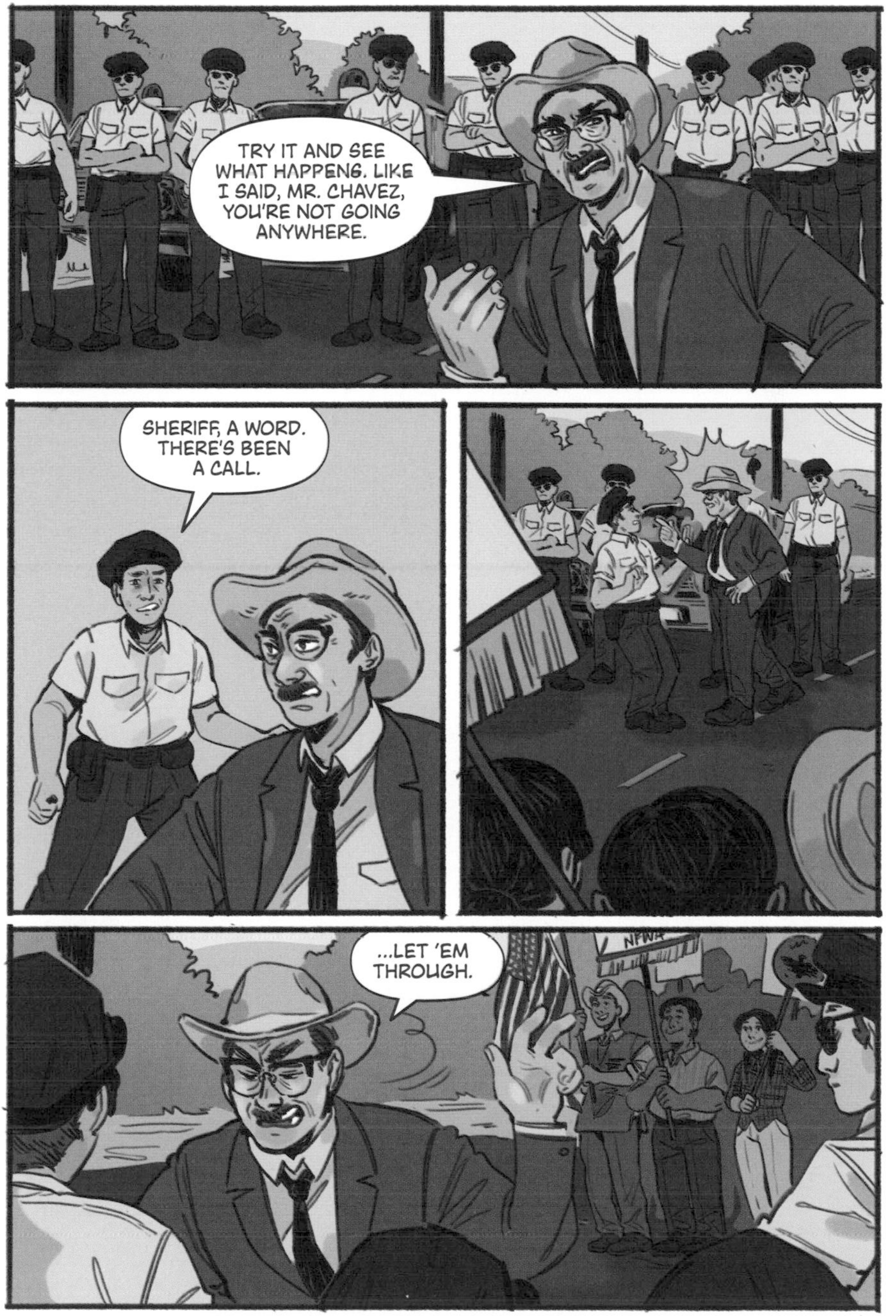
TRY IT AND SEE WHAT HAPPENS. LIKE I SAID, MR. CHAVEZ, YOU'RE NOT GOING ANYWHERE.
SHERIFF, A WORD. THERE'S BEEN A CALL.
...LET 'EM THROUGH.
NFWA

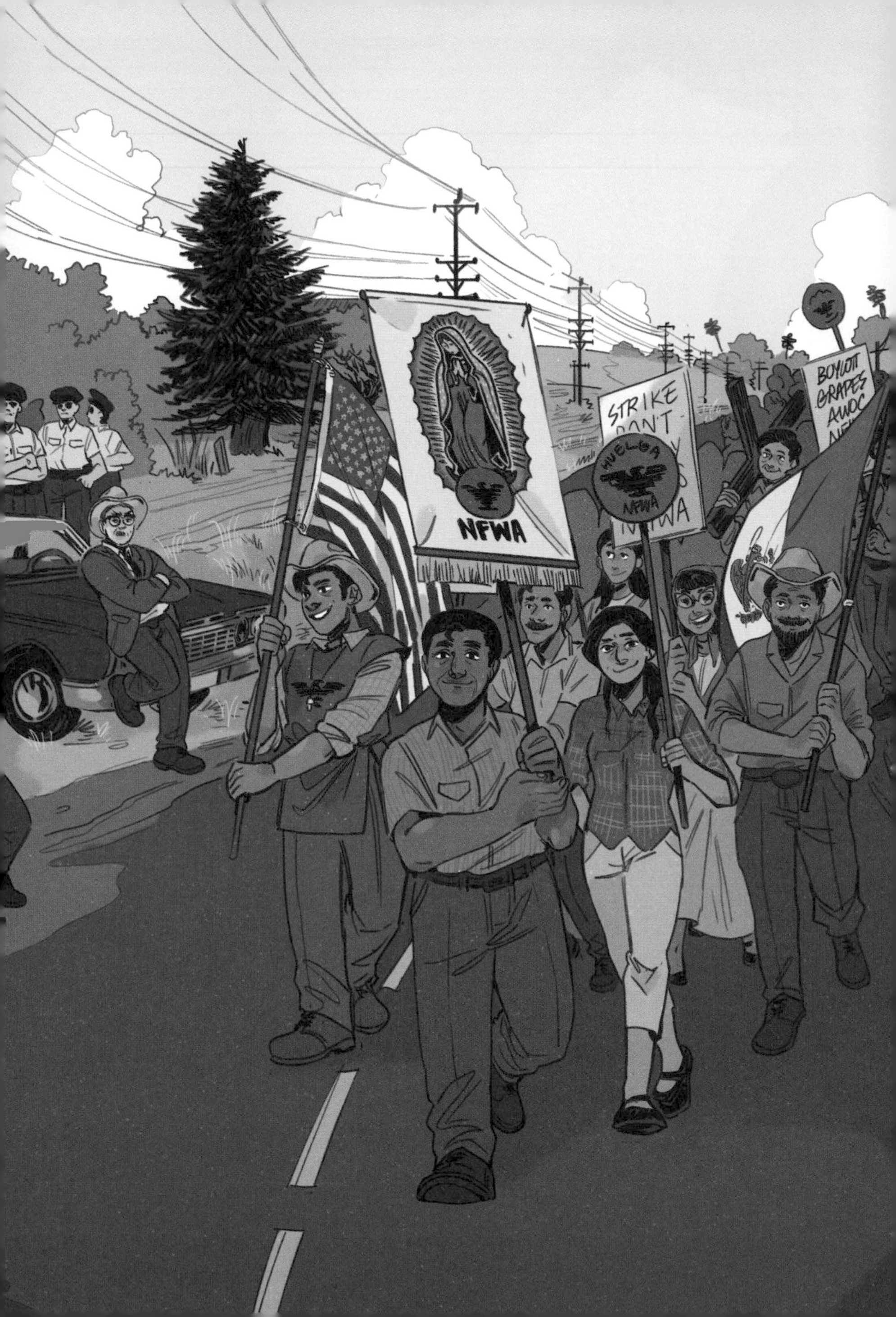

NFWA
STRIKE
HUELGA
NFWA
BOYCOTT
GRAPES
AWOC

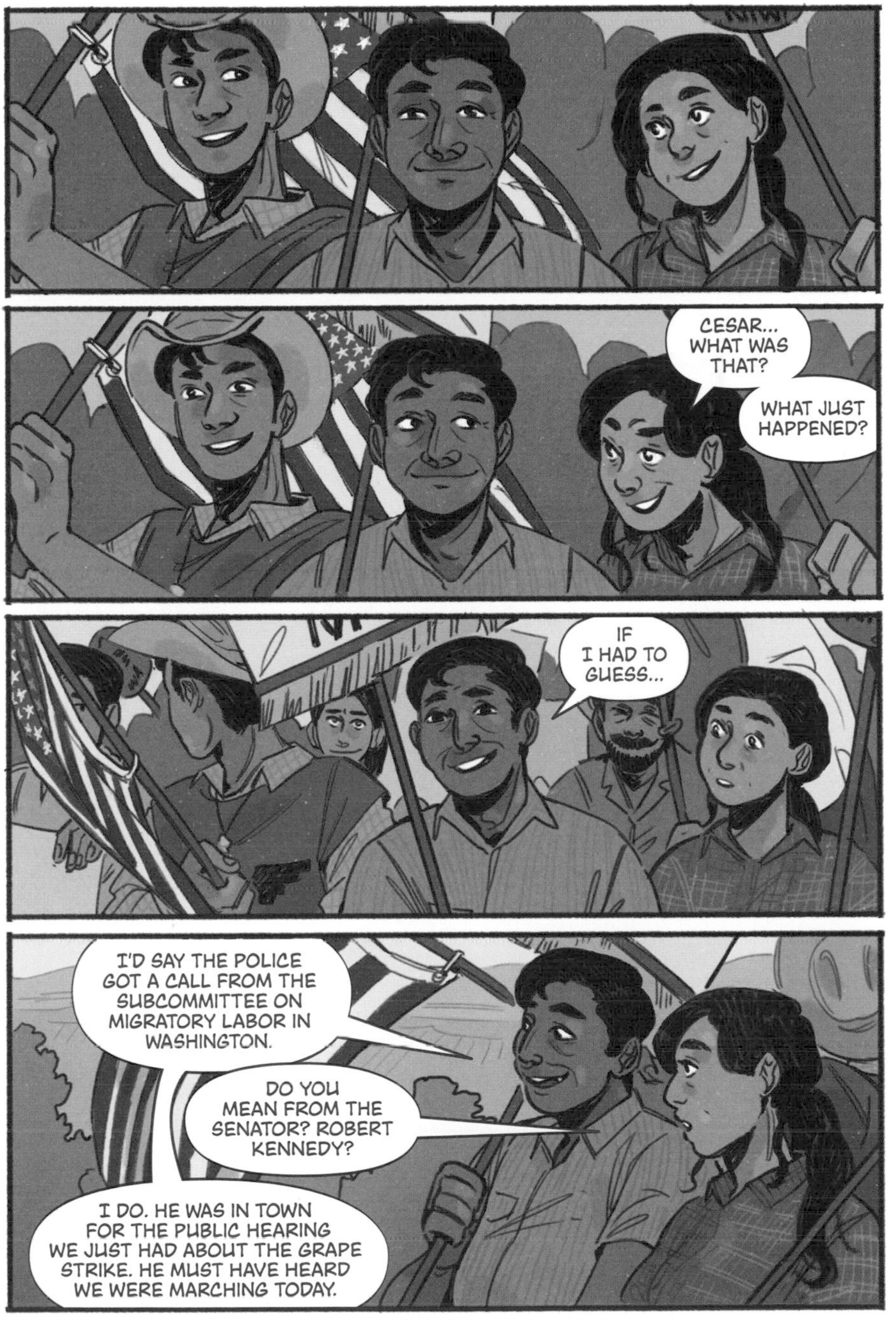
CESAR... WHAT WAS THAT?
WHAT JUST HAPPENED?
IF I HAD TO GUESS...
I'D SAY THE POLICE GOT A CALL FROM THE SUBCOMMITTEE ON MIGRATORY LABOR IN WASHINGTON.
DO YOU MEAN FROM THE SENATOR? ROBERT KENNEDY?
I DO. HE WAS IN TOWN FOR THE PUBLIC HEARING WE JUST HAD ABOUT THE GRAPE STRIKE. HE MUST HAVE HEARD WE WERE MARCHING TODAY.

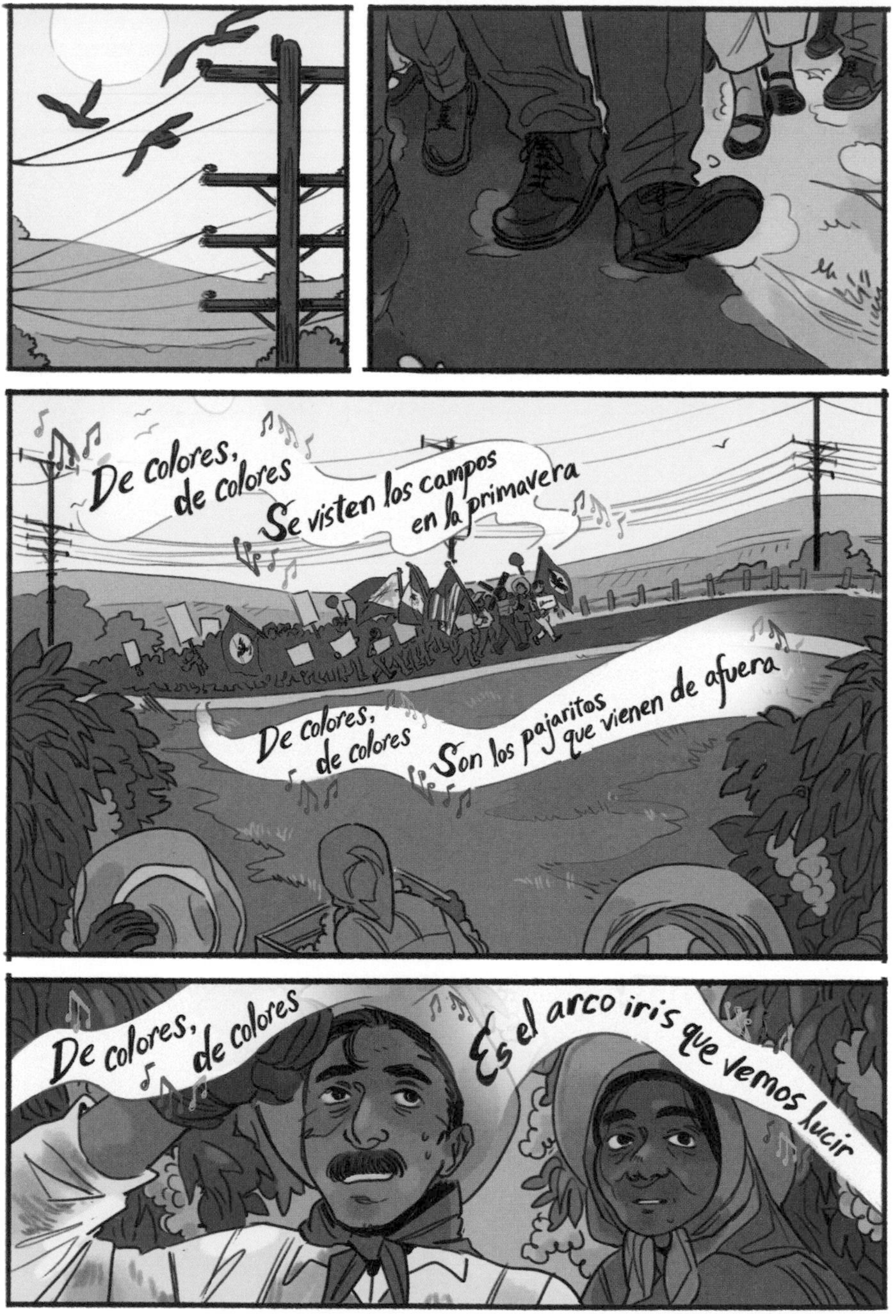
De colores, de colores
Se visten los campos en la primavera
De colores, de colores
Son los pajaritos que vienen de afuera
De colores, de colores
Es el arco iris que vemos lucir

The March from Delano to Sacramento

One of the most crucial moments of the Delano Grape Strike was a march from the city of Delano in Southern California up to Sacramento, which is California's capital city. The distance between the two cities is about 245 miles, but rather than walking directly to Sacramento, the marchers felt they should visit towns and farms along the way to get more farmworkers to join their cause.

As the number of marchers grew, many things needed to be taken into account, such as food, water, bathroom breaks, and sleeping accommodations. This made the march 340 miles long. Eventually, they went through 53 towns and stayed overnight in half. Some of the other towns they visited and passed through were: Richgrove, Ducor, Terra Bella, Porterville, Lindsay, Farmersville, Visalia, Dinuba, Reedley, Sanger, and Selma.

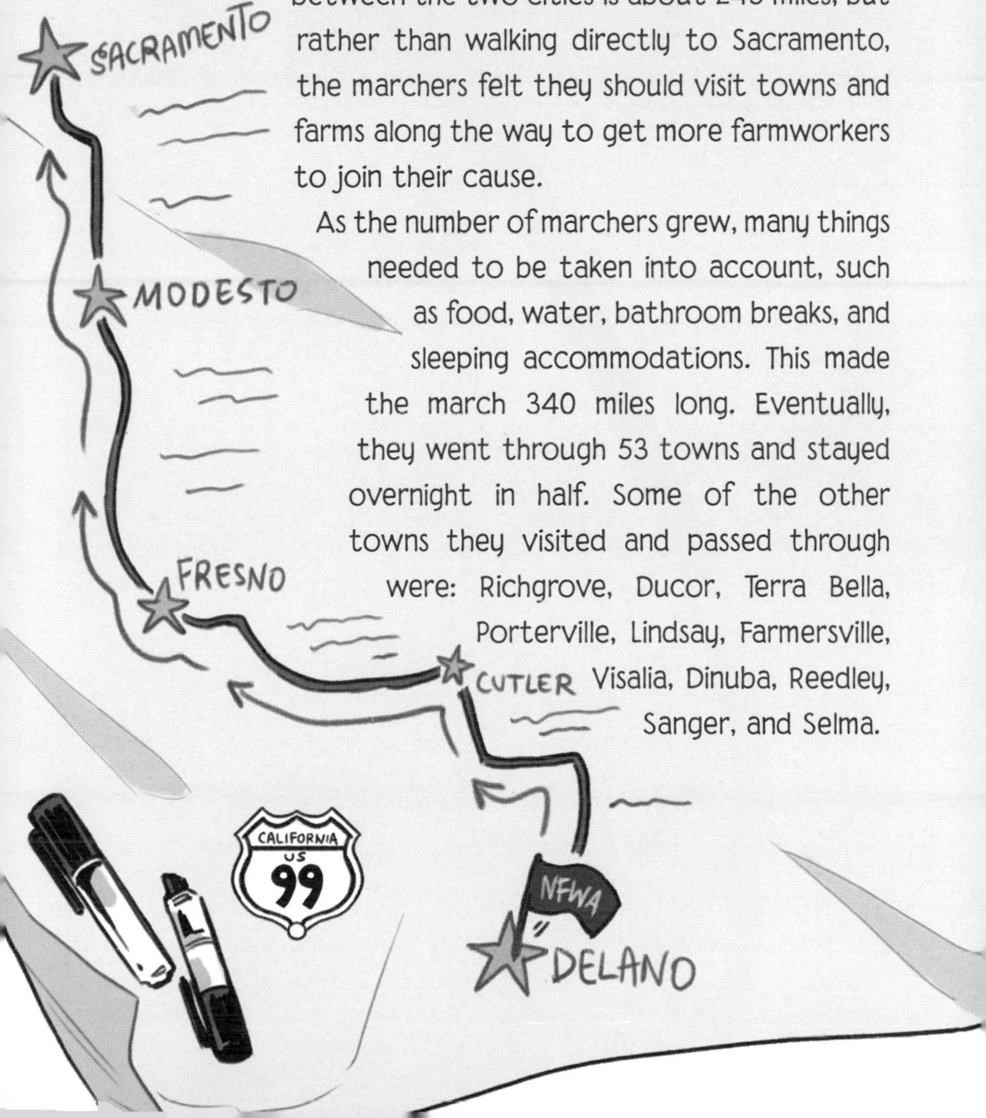
SACRAMENTO
MODESTO
FRESNO
CUTLER
CALIFORNIA
US
99
NFWA
DELANO

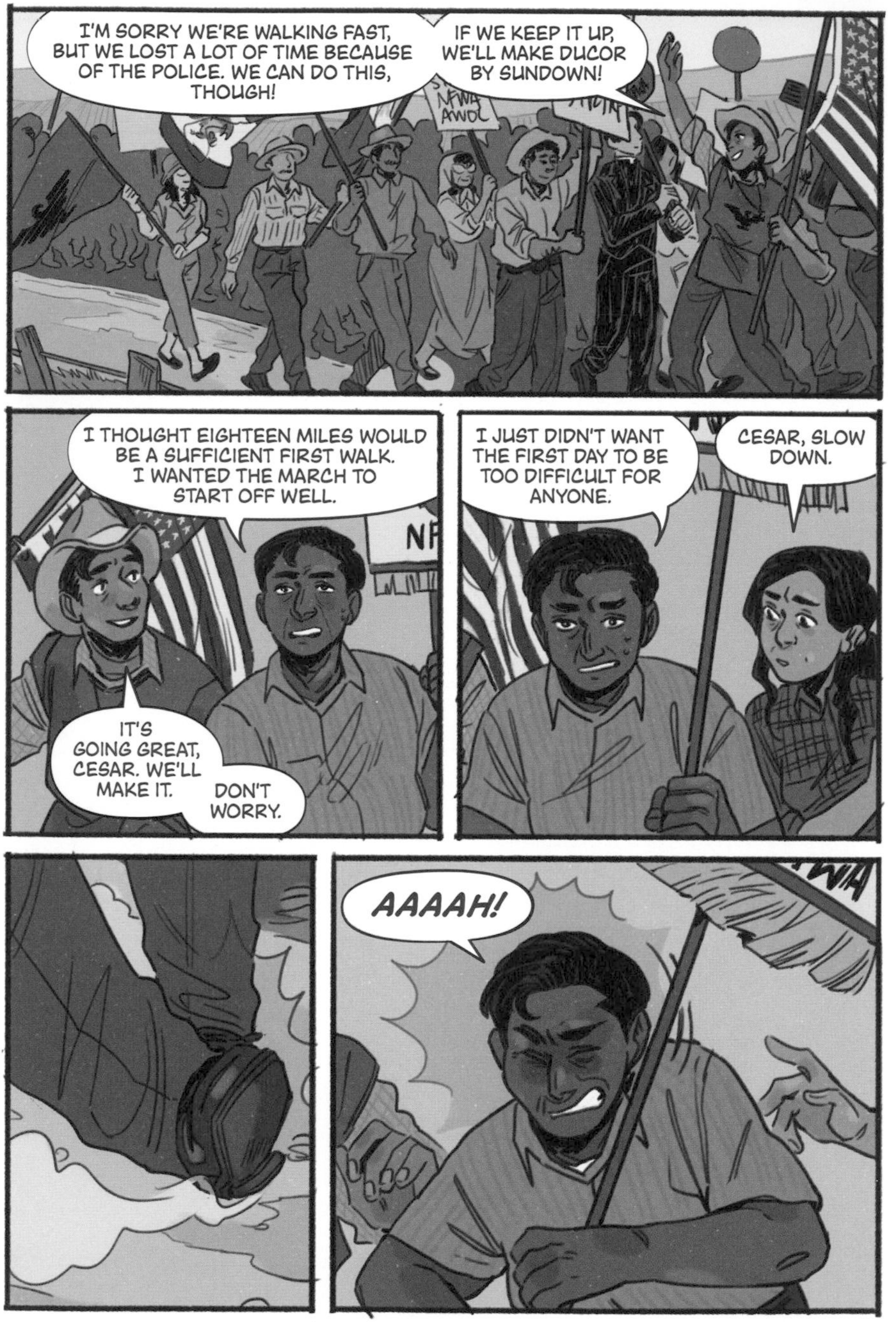
I'M SORRY WE'RE WALKING FAST, BUT WE LOST A LOT OF TIME BECAUSE OF THE POLICE. WE CAN DO THIS, THOUGH!
IF WE KEEP IT UP, WE'LL MAKE DUCOR BY SUNDOWN!
NFWA
AWOC
I THOUGHT EIGHTEEN MILES WOULD BE A SUFFICIENT FIRST WALK. I WANTED THE MARCH TO START OFF WELL.
IT'S GOING GREAT, CESAR. WE'LL MAKE IT.
DON'T WORRY.
I JUST DIDN'T WANT THE FIRST DAY TO BE TOO DIFFICULT FOR ANYONE.
CESAR, SLOW DOWN.
AAAAH!

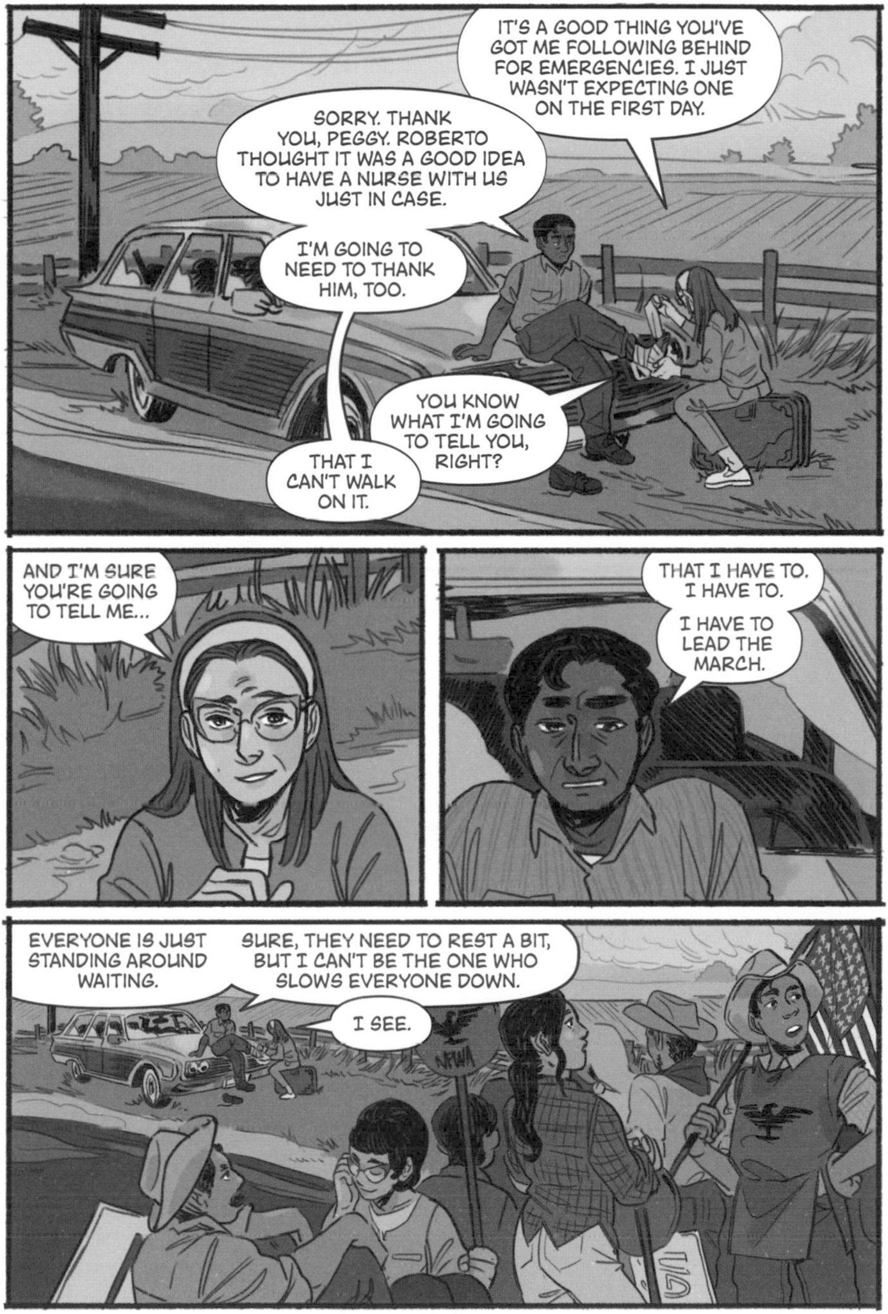
IT'S A GOOD THING YOU'VE GOT ME FOLLOWING BEHIND FOR EMERGENCIES. I JUST WASN'T EXPECTING ONE ON THE FIRST DAY.
SORRY. THANK YOU, PEGGY. ROBERTO THOUGHT IT WAS A GOOD IDEA TO HAVE A NURSE WITH US JUST IN CASE.
I'M GOING TO NEED TO THANK HIM, TOO.
YOU KNOW WHAT I'M GOING TO TELL YOU, RIGHT?
THAT I CAN'T WALK ON IT.
AND I'M SURE YOU'RE GOING TO TELL ME...
THAT I HAVE TO. I HAVE TO.
I HAVE TO LEAD THE MARCH.
EVERYONE IS JUST STANDING AROUND WAITING.
SURE, THEY NEED TO REST A BIT, BUT I CAN'T BE THE ONE WHO SLOWS EVERYONE DOWN.
I SEE.
NFWA

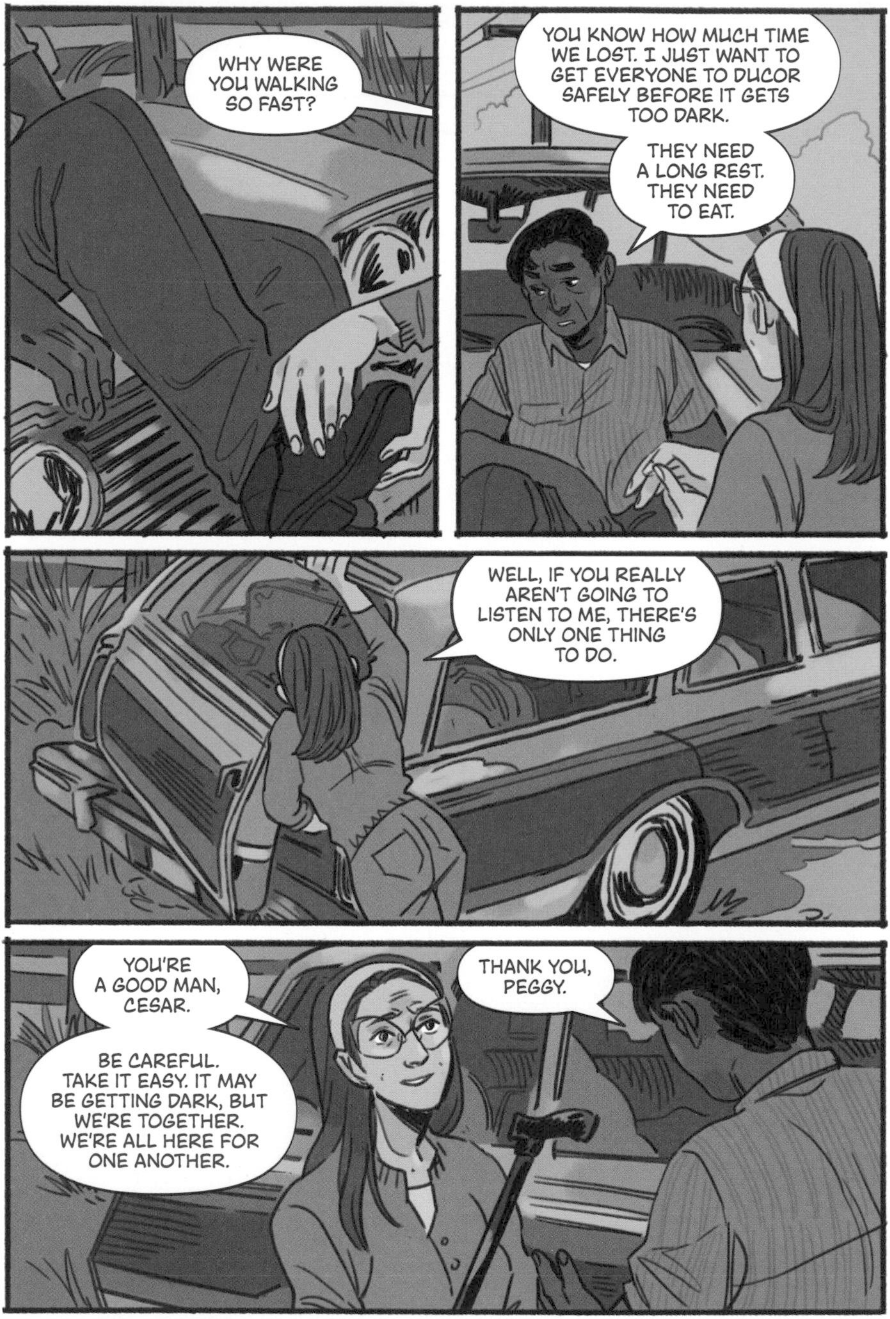
WHY WERE YOU WALKING SO FAST?
YOU KNOW HOW MUCH TIME WE LOST. I JUST WANT TO GET EVERYONE TO DUCOR SAFELY BEFORE IT GETS TOO DARK.
THEY NEED A LONG REST. THEY NEED TO EAT.
WELL, IF YOU REALLY AREN'T GOING TO LISTEN TO ME, THERE'S ONLY ONE THING TO DO.
YOU'RE A GOOD MAN, CESAR.
THANK YOU, PEGGY.
BE CAREFUL. TAKE IT EASY. IT MAY BE GETTING DARK, BUT WE'RE TOGETHER. WE'RE ALL HERE FOR ONE ANOTHER.

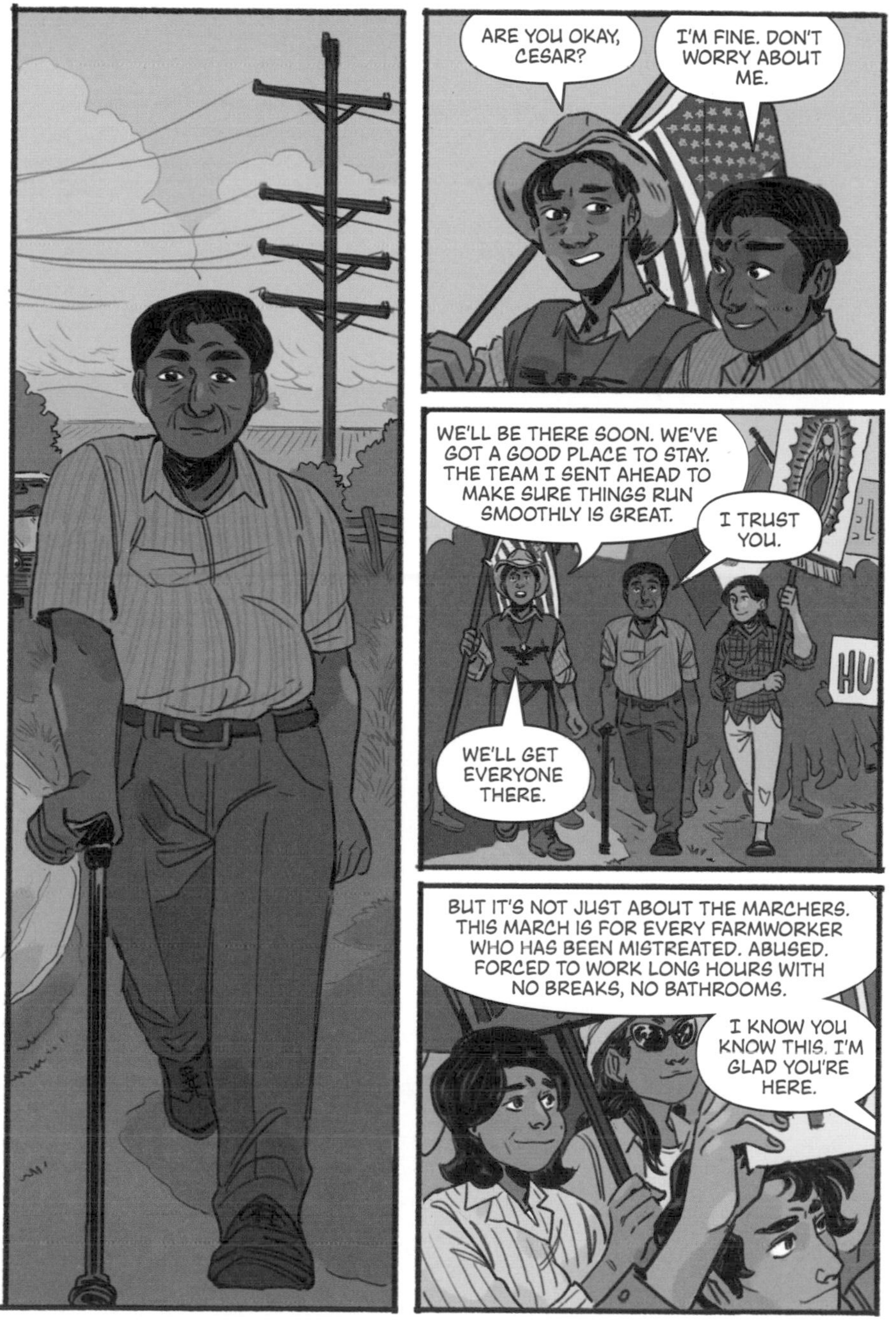
ARE YOU OKAY, CESAR?
I'M FINE. DON'T WORRY ABOUT ME.
WE'LL BE THERE SOON. WE'VE GOT A GOOD PLACE TO STAY. THE TEAM I SENT AHEAD TO MAKE SURE THINGS RUN SMOOTHLY IS GREAT.
I TRUST YOU.
WE'LL GET EVERYONE THERE.
HU
BUT IT'S NOT JUST ABOUT THE MARCHERS. THIS MARCH IS FOR EVERY FARMWORKER WHO HAS BEEN MISTREATED. ABUSED. FORCED TO WORK LONG HOURS WITH NO BREAKS, NO BATHROOMS.
I KNOW YOU KNOW THIS. I'M GLAD YOU'RE HERE.

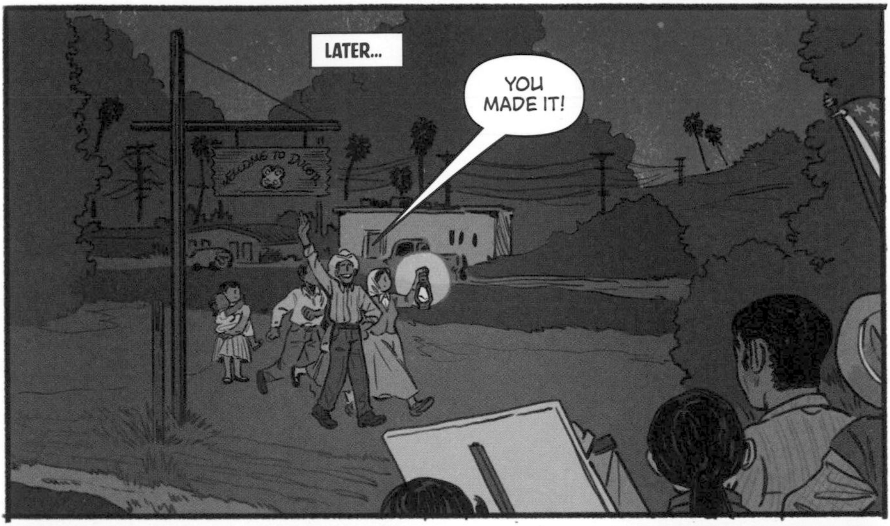
LATER...
YOU MADE IT!

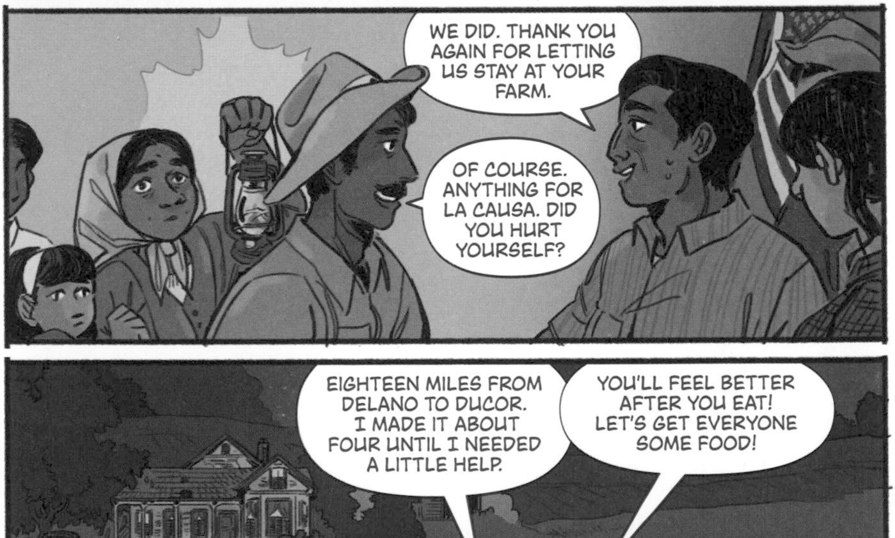
WE DID. THANK YOU AGAIN FOR LETTING US STAY AT YOUR FARM.
OF COURSE. ANYTHING FOR LA CAUSA. DID YOU HURT YOURSELF?

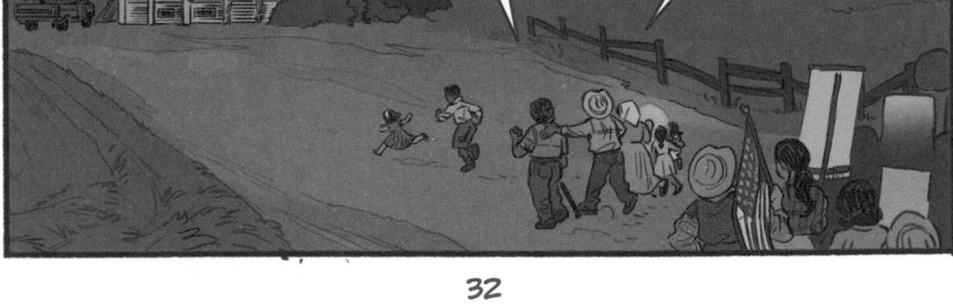
EIGHTEEN MILES FROM DELANO TO DUCOR. I MADE IT ABOUT FOUR UNTIL I NEEDED A LITTLE HELP.
YOU'LL FEEL BETTER AFTER YOU EAT! LET'S GET EVERYONE SOME FOOD!

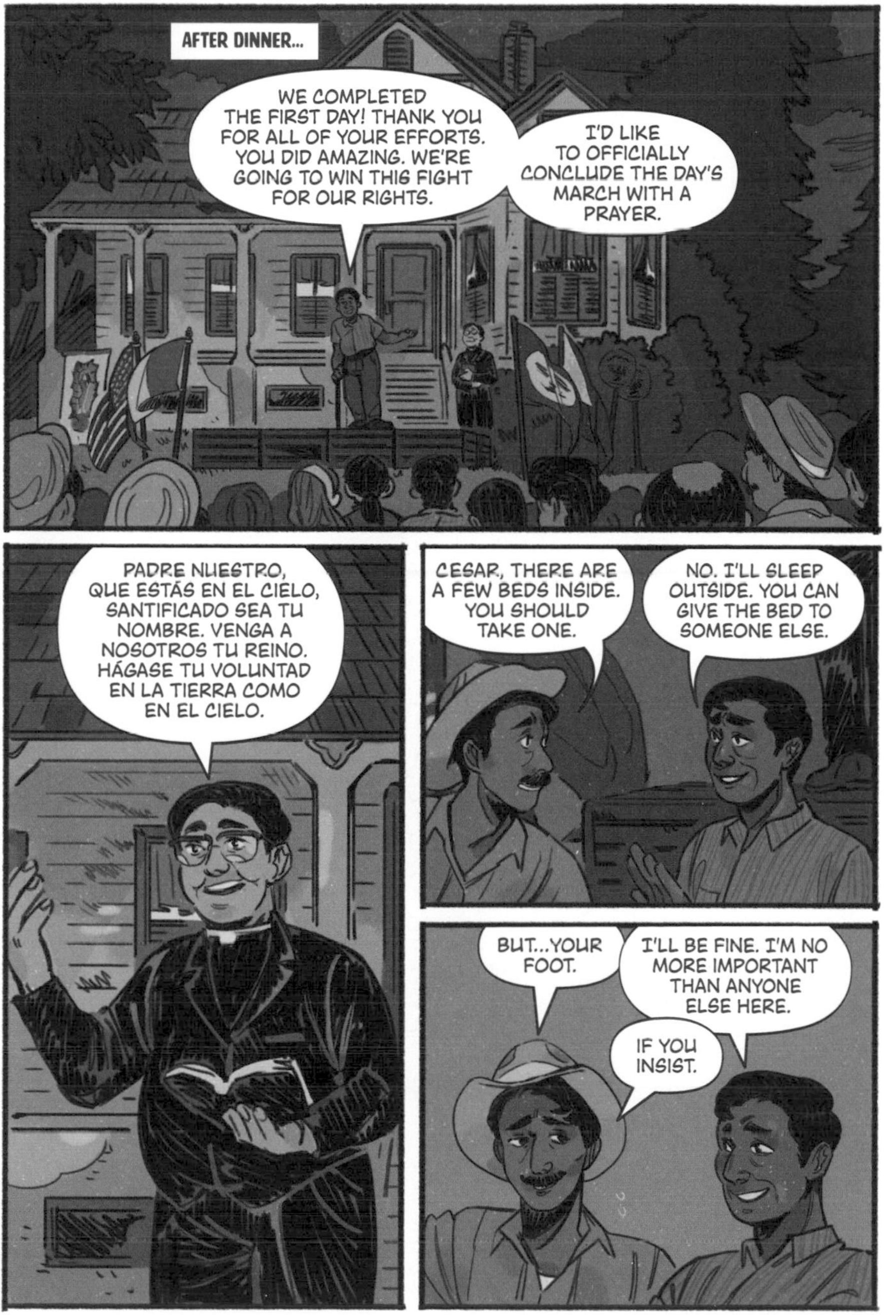
AFTER DINNER...
WE COMPLETED THE FIRST DAY! THANK YOU FOR ALL OF YOUR EFFORTS. YOU DID AMAZING. WE'RE GOING TO WIN THIS FIGHT FOR OUR RIGHTS.
I'D LIKE TO OFFICIALLY CONCLUDE THE DAY'S MARCH WITH A PRAYER.
PADRE NUESTRO, QUE ESTÁS EN EL CIELO, SANTIFICADO SEA TU NOMBRE. VENGA A NOSOTROS TU REINO. HÁGASE TU VOLUNTAD EN LA TIERRA COMO EN EL CIELO.
CESAR, THERE ARE A FEW BEDS INSIDE. YOU SHOULD TAKE ONE.
NO. I'LL SLEEP OUTSIDE. YOU CAN GIVE THE BED TO SOMEONE ELSE.
BUT...YOUR FOOT.
I'LL BE FINE. I'M NO MORE IMPORTANT THAN ANYONE ELSE HERE.
IF YOU INSIST.

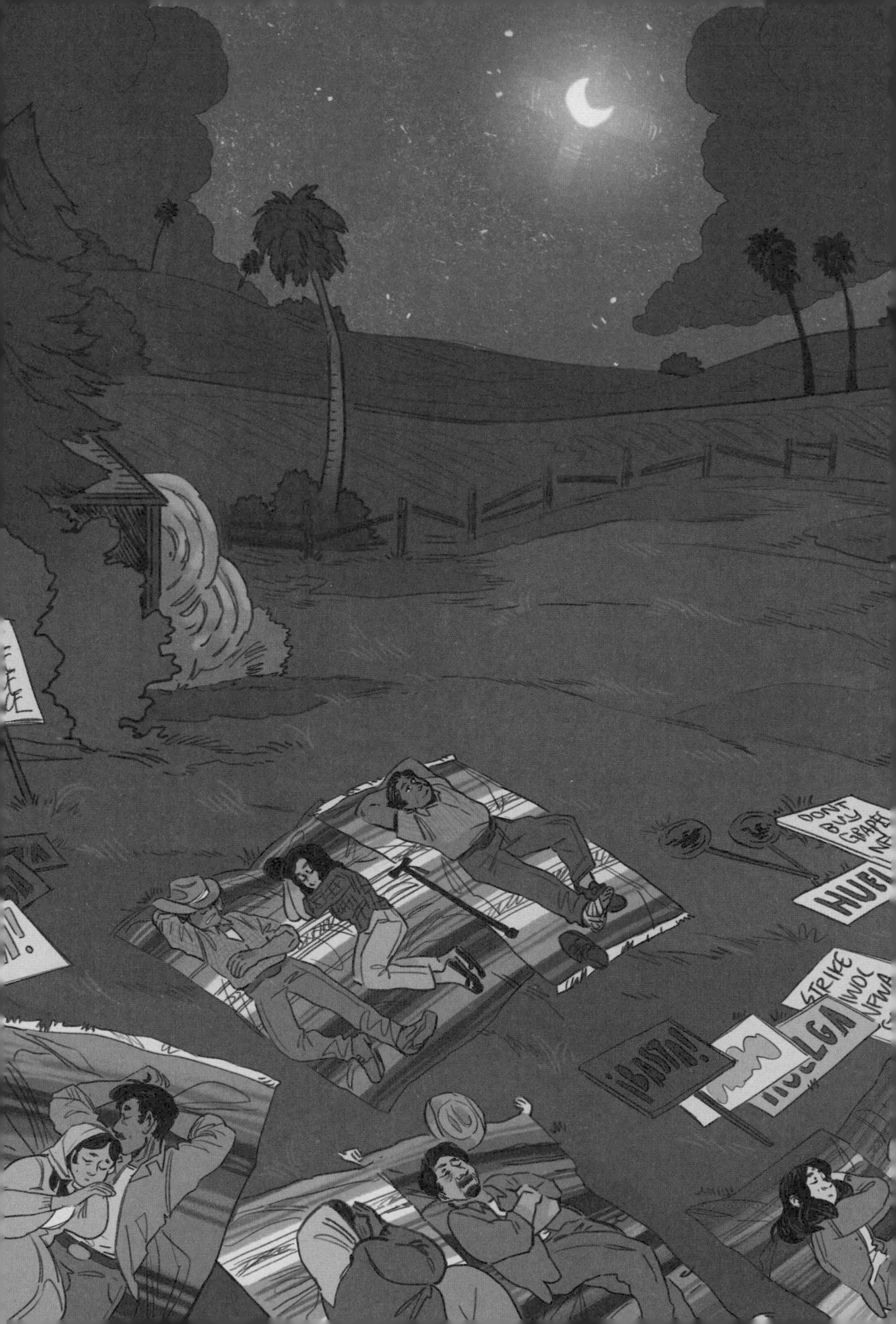
DONT BUY GRAPE
HUEL
STRIKE
IWOC
NFWA
¡BASTA!
LGA

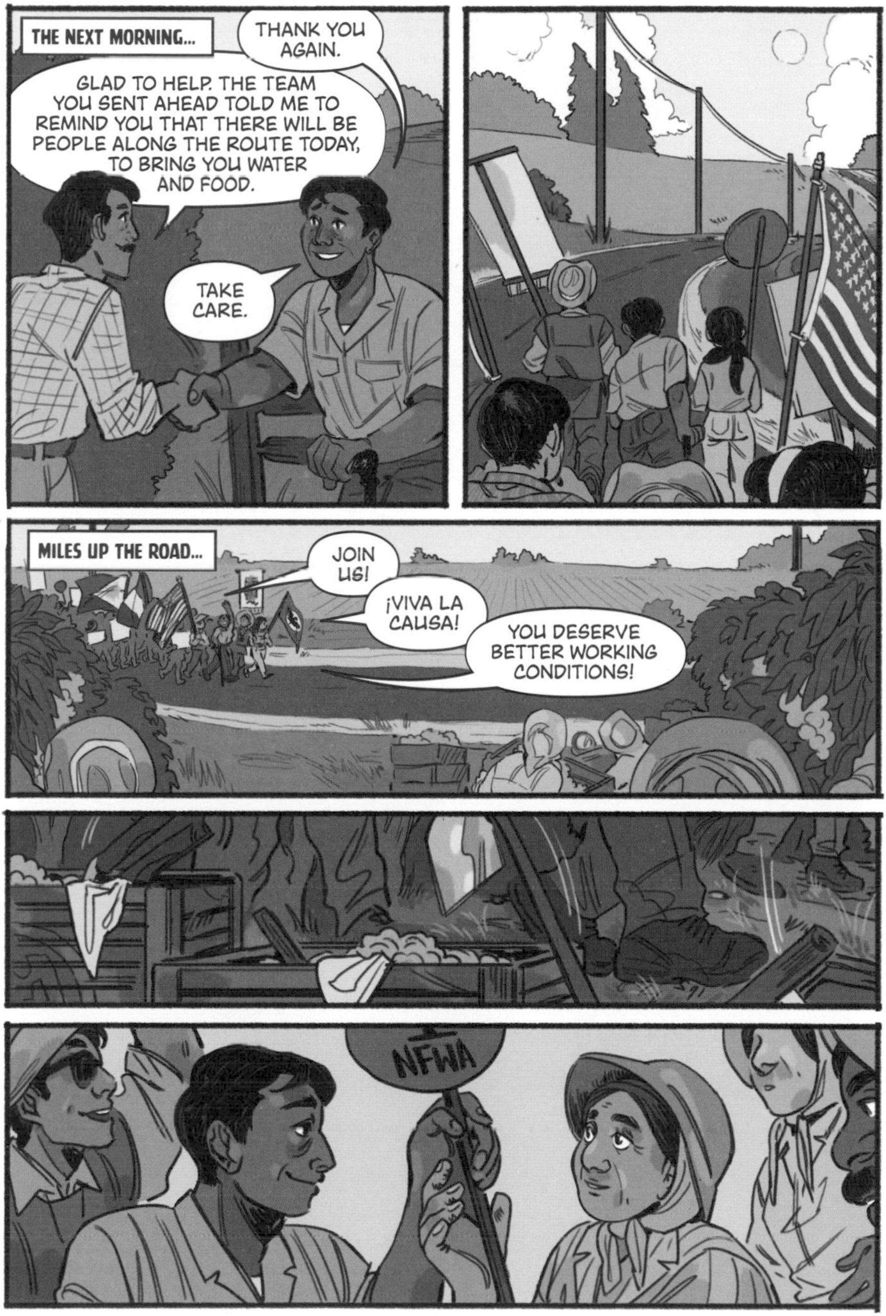

THE NEXT MORNING...
THANK YOU AGAIN.
GLAD TO HELP. THE TEAM YOU SENT AHEAD TOLD ME TO REMIND YOU THAT THERE WILL BE PEOPLE ALONG THE ROUTE TODAY, TO BRING YOU WATER AND FOOD.
TAKE CARE.
MILES UP THE ROAD...
JOIN US!
¡VIVA LA CAUSA!
YOU DESERVE BETTER WORKING CONDITIONS!
NFWA

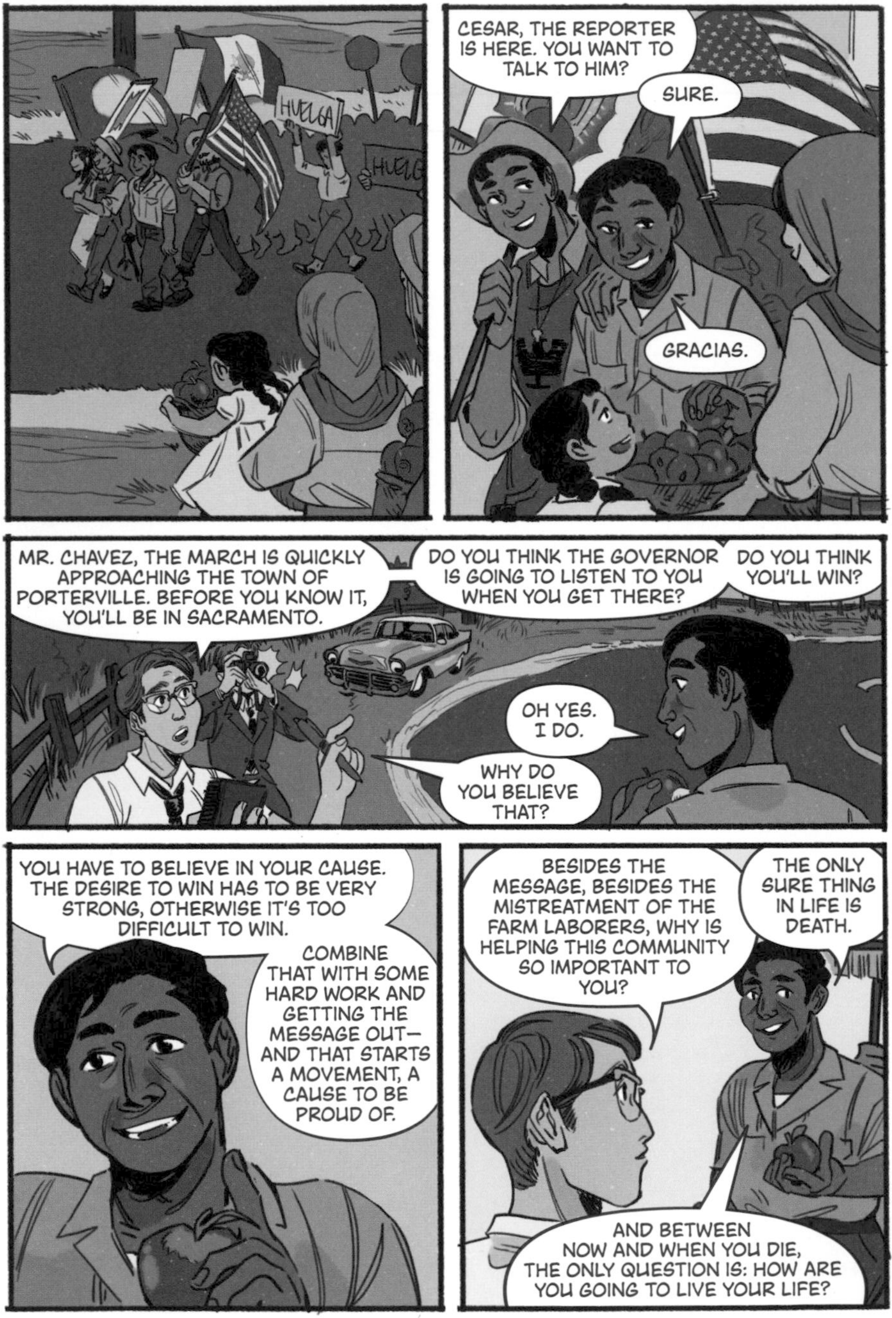
HUELGA
HUELGA
CESAR, THE REPORTER IS HERE. YOU WANT TO TALK TO HIM?
SURE.
GRACIAS.
MR. CHAVEZ, THE MARCH IS QUICKLY APPROACHING THE TOWN OF PORTERVILLE. BEFORE YOU KNOW IT, YOU'LL BE IN SACRAMENTO.
DO YOU THINK THE GOVERNOR IS GOING TO LISTEN TO YOU WHEN YOU GET THERE?
DO YOU THINK YOU'LL WIN?
OH YES. I DO.
WHY DO YOU BELIEVE THAT?
YOU HAVE TO BELIEVE IN YOUR CAUSE. THE DESIRE TO WIN HAS TO BE VERY STRONG, OTHERWISE IT'S TOO DIFFICULT TO WIN.
COMBINE THAT WITH SOME HARD WORK AND GETTING THE MESSAGE OUT—AND THAT STARTS A MOVEMENT, A CAUSE TO BE PROUD OF.
BESIDES THE MESSAGE, BESIDES THE MISTREATMENT OF THE FARM LABORERS, WHY IS HELPING THIS COMMUNITY SO IMPORTANT TO YOU?
THE ONLY SURE THING IN LIFE IS DEATH.
AND BETWEEN NOW AND WHEN YOU DIE, THE ONLY QUESTION IS: HOW ARE YOU GOING TO LIVE YOUR LIFE?

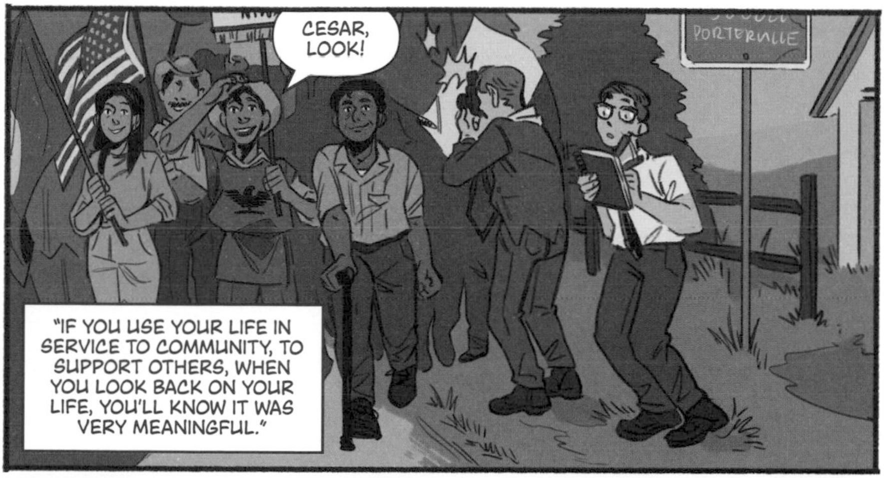
CESAR, LOOK!
PORTERVILLE
"IF YOU USE YOUR LIFE IN SERVICE TO COMMUNITY, TO SUPPORT OTHERS, WHEN YOU LOOK BACK ON YOUR LIFE, YOU'LL KNOW IT WAS VERY MEANINGFUL."

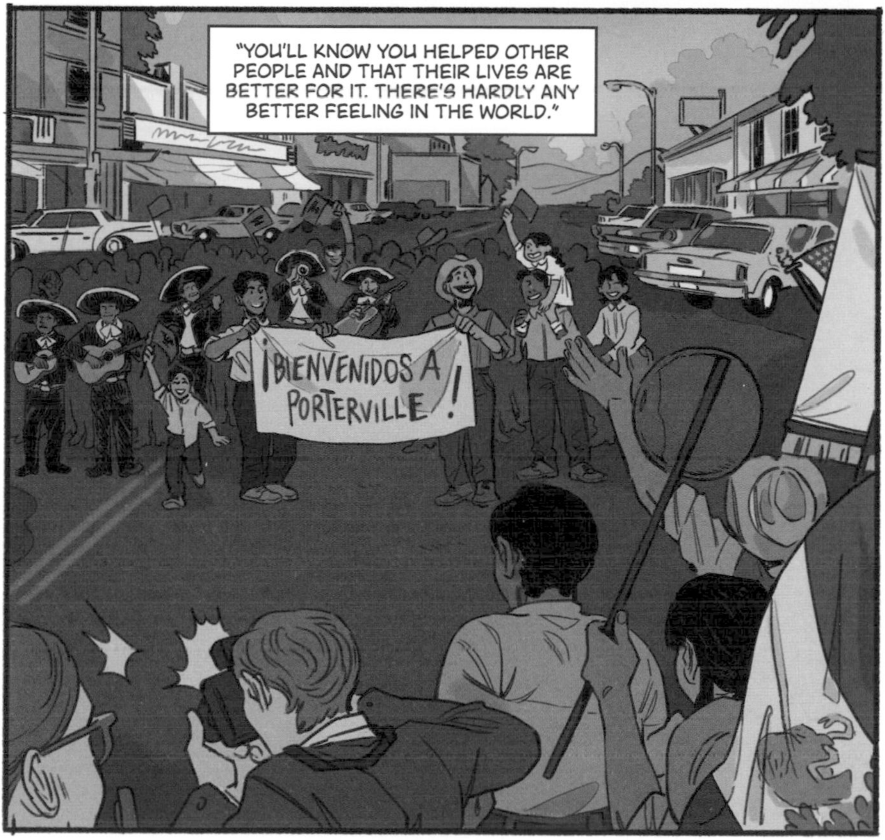
"YOU'LL KNOW YOU HELPED OTHER PEOPLE AND THAT THEIR LIVES ARE BETTER FOR IT. THERE'S HARDLY ANY BETTER FEELING IN THE WORLD."
¡BIENVENIDOS A PORTERVILLE!

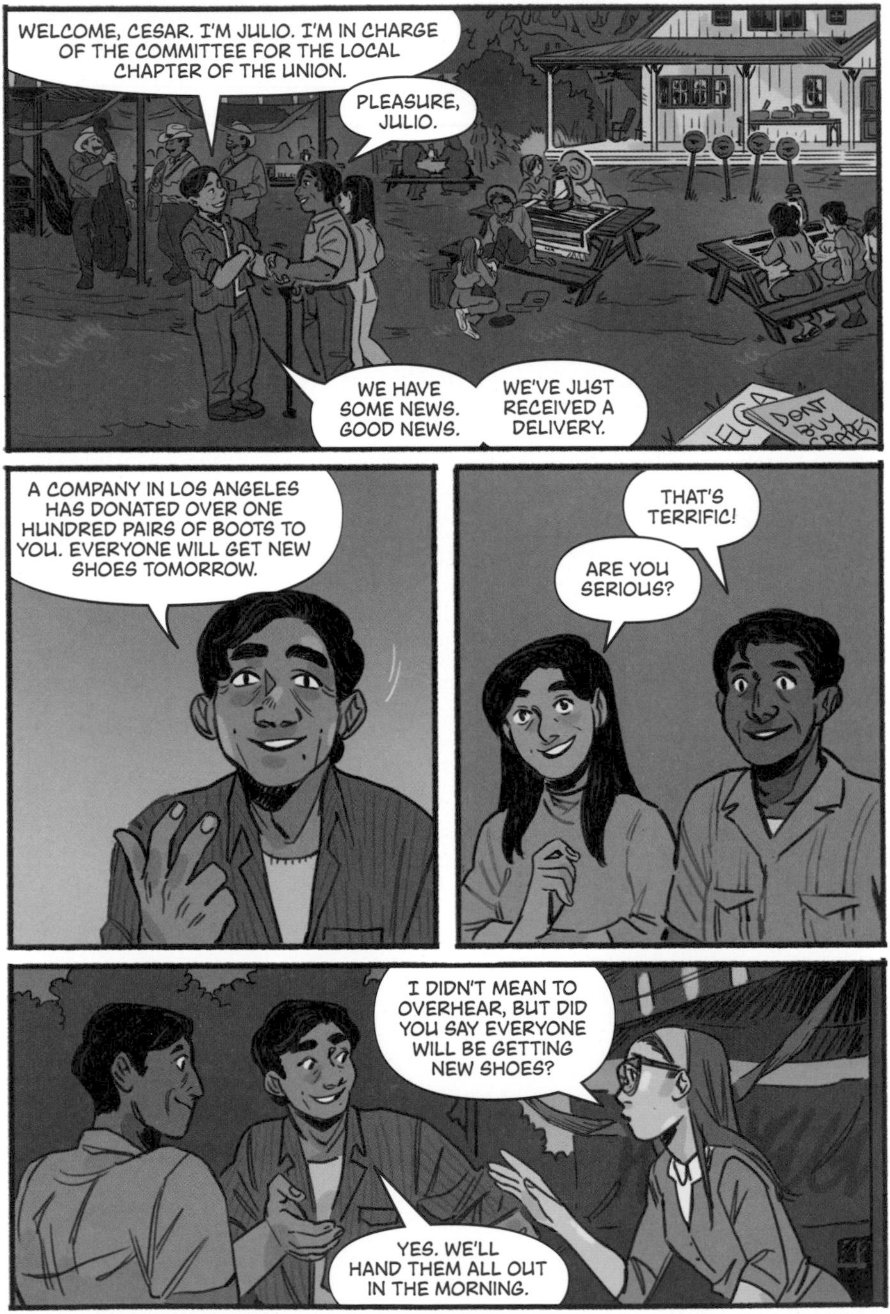
WELCOME, CESAR. I'M JULIO. I'M IN CHARGE OF THE COMMITTEE FOR THE LOCAL CHAPTER OF THE UNION.
PLEASURE, JULIO.
WE HAVE SOME NEWS. GOOD NEWS.
WE'VE JUST RECEIVED A DELIVERY.
A COMPANY IN LOS ANGELES HAS DONATED OVER ONE HUNDRED PAIRS OF BOOTS TO YOU. EVERYONE WILL GET NEW SHOES TOMORROW.
THAT'S TERRIFIC!
ARE YOU SERIOUS?
I DIDN'T MEAN TO OVERHEAR, BUT DID YOU SAY EVERYONE WILL BE GETTING NEW SHOES?
YES. WE'LL HAND THEM ALL OUT IN THE MORNING.

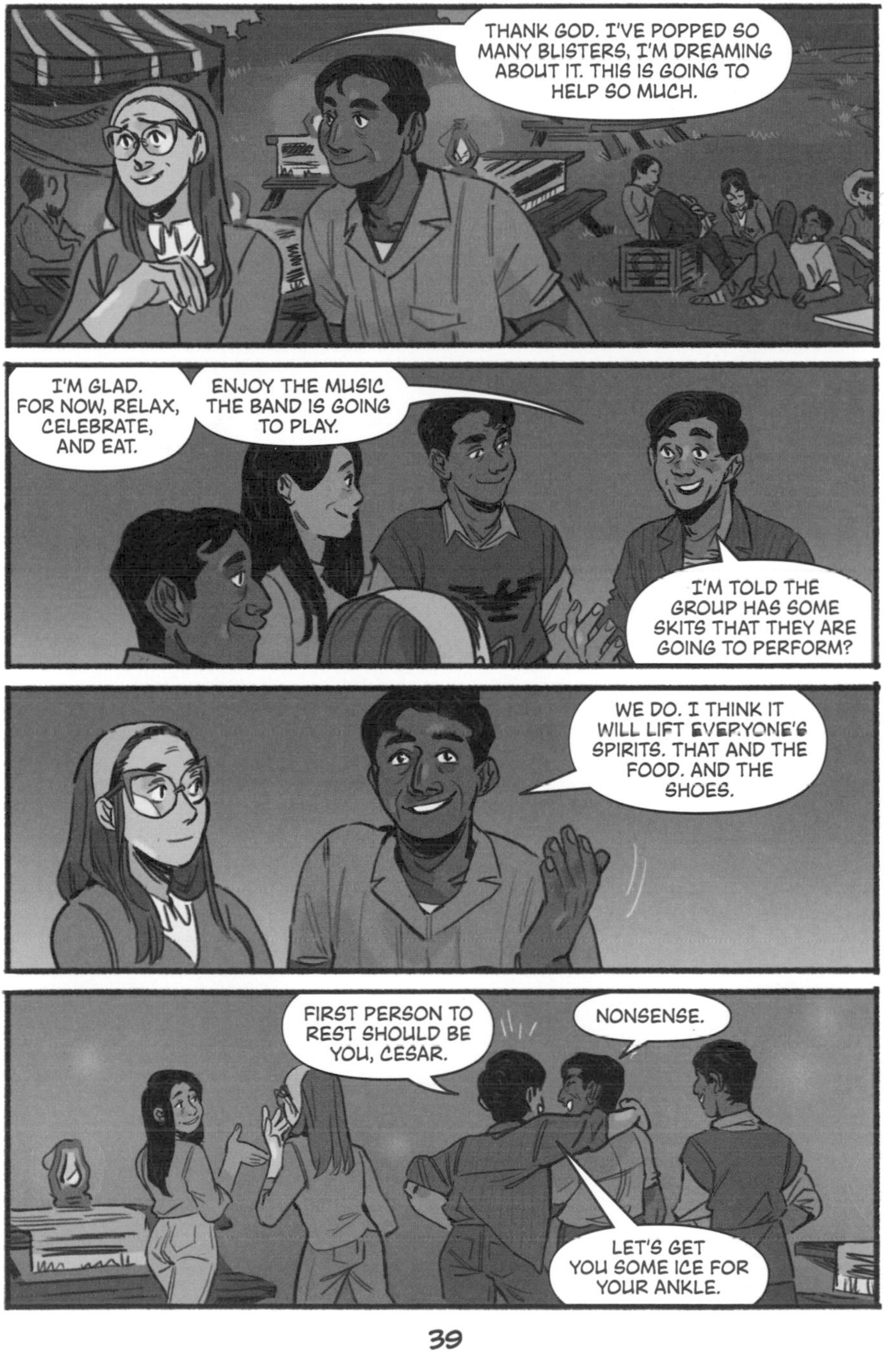
THANK GOD. I'VE POPPED SO MANY BLISTERS, I'M DREAMING ABOUT IT. THIS IS GOING TO HELP SO MUCH.
I'M GLAD. FOR NOW, RELAX, CELEBRATE, AND EAT.
ENJOY THE MUSIC THE BAND IS GOING TO PLAY.
I'M TOLD THE GROUP HAS SOME SKITS THAT THEY ARE GOING TO PERFORM?
WE DO. I THINK IT WILL LIFT EVERYONE'S SPIRITS. THAT AND THE FOOD. AND THE SHOES.
FIRST PERSON TO REST SHOULD BE YOU, CESAR.
NONSENSE.
LET'S GET YOU SOME ICE FOR YOUR ANKLE.

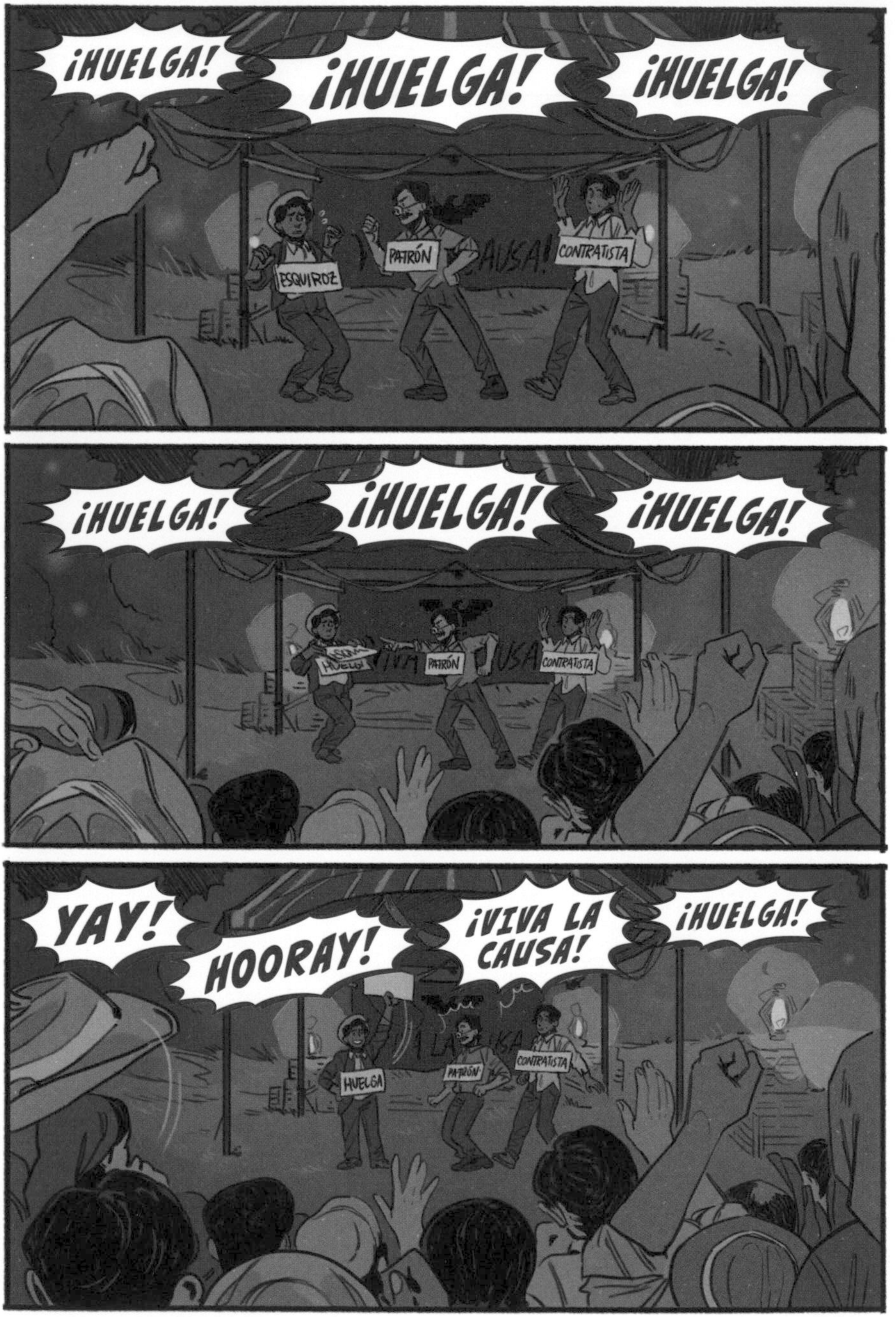
¡HUELGA!
¡HUELGA!
¡HUELGA!
ESQUIROZ
PATRÓN
CONTRATISTA
¡HUELGA!
¡HUELGA!
¡HUELGA!
PATRÓN
CONTRATISTA
YAY!
HOORAY!
¡VIVA LA CAUSA!
¡HUELGA!
HUELGA
PATRÓN
CONTRATISTA

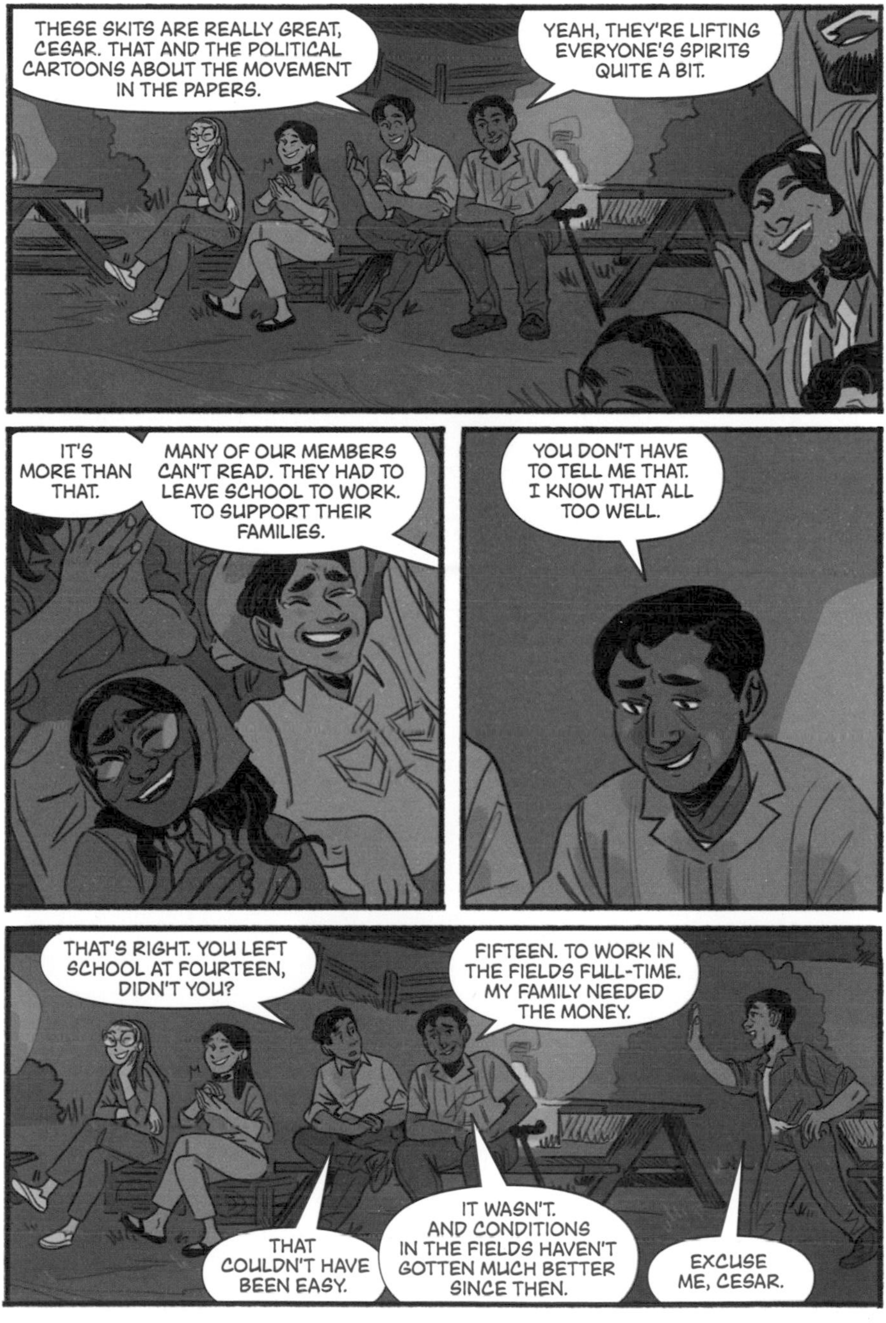
THESE SKITS ARE REALLY GREAT, CESAR. THAT AND THE POLITICAL CARTOONS ABOUT THE MOVEMENT IN THE PAPERS.
YEAH, THEY'RE LIFTING EVERYONE'S SPIRITS QUITE A BIT.
IT'S MORE THAN THAT.
MANY OF OUR MEMBERS CAN'T READ. THEY HAD TO LEAVE SCHOOL TO WORK. TO SUPPORT THEIR FAMILIES.
YOU DON'T HAVE TO TELL ME THAT. I KNOW THAT ALL TOO WELL.
THAT'S RIGHT. YOU LEFT SCHOOL AT FOURTEEN, DIDN'T YOU?
FIFTEEN. TO WORK IN THE FIELDS FULL-TIME. MY FAMILY NEEDED THE MONEY.
THAT COULDN'T HAVE BEEN EASY.
IT WASN'T. AND CONDITIONS IN THE FIELDS HAVEN'T GOTTEN MUCH BETTER SINCE THEN.
EXCUSE ME, CESAR.

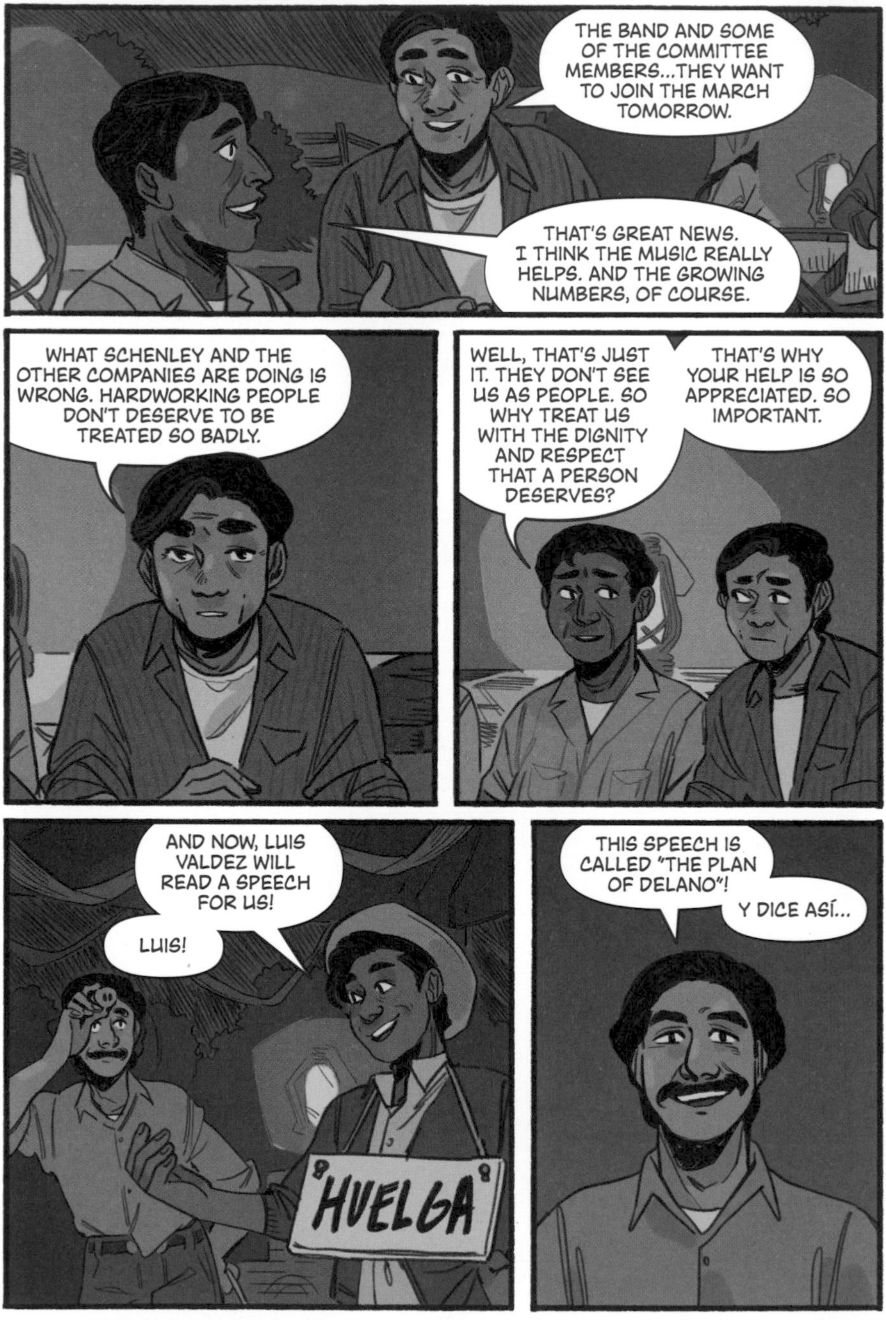
THE BAND AND SOME OF THE COMMITTEE MEMBERS...THEY WANT TO JOIN THE MARCH TOMORROW.
THAT'S GREAT NEWS. I THINK THE MUSIC REALLY HELPS. AND THE GROWING NUMBERS, OF COURSE.
WHAT SCHENLEY AND THE OTHER COMPANIES ARE DOING IS WRONG. HARDWORKING PEOPLE DON'T DESERVE TO BE TREATED SO BADLY.
WELL, THAT'S JUST IT. THEY DON'T SEE US AS PEOPLE. SO WHY TREAT US WITH THE DIGNITY AND RESPECT THAT A PERSON DESERVES?
THAT'S WHY YOUR HELP IS SO APPRECIATED. SO IMPORTANT.
AND NOW, LUIS VALDEZ WILL READ A SPEECH FOR US!
LUIS!
HUELGA
THIS SPEECH IS CALLED "THE PLAN OF DELANO"!
Y DICE ASÍ...

El Plan de Delano

"El Plan de Delano" was a speech that Cesar wrote together with Luis Valdez, an American playwright, actor, and film director. It was inspired by "El Plan de Ayala," a speech written by the followers of Emiliano Zapata, who was a leading figure in the Mexican Revolution. "El Plan de Delano" was meant to be read every night of the march to help unify the marchers and remind them of their purpose to fight for workers' rights. Cesar felt it was important that the speech was focused on actions and not words. The speech spoke of uniting, striking, and overcoming the injustices the farmworkers experienced.

The speech was completed just days before the march to Sacramento.

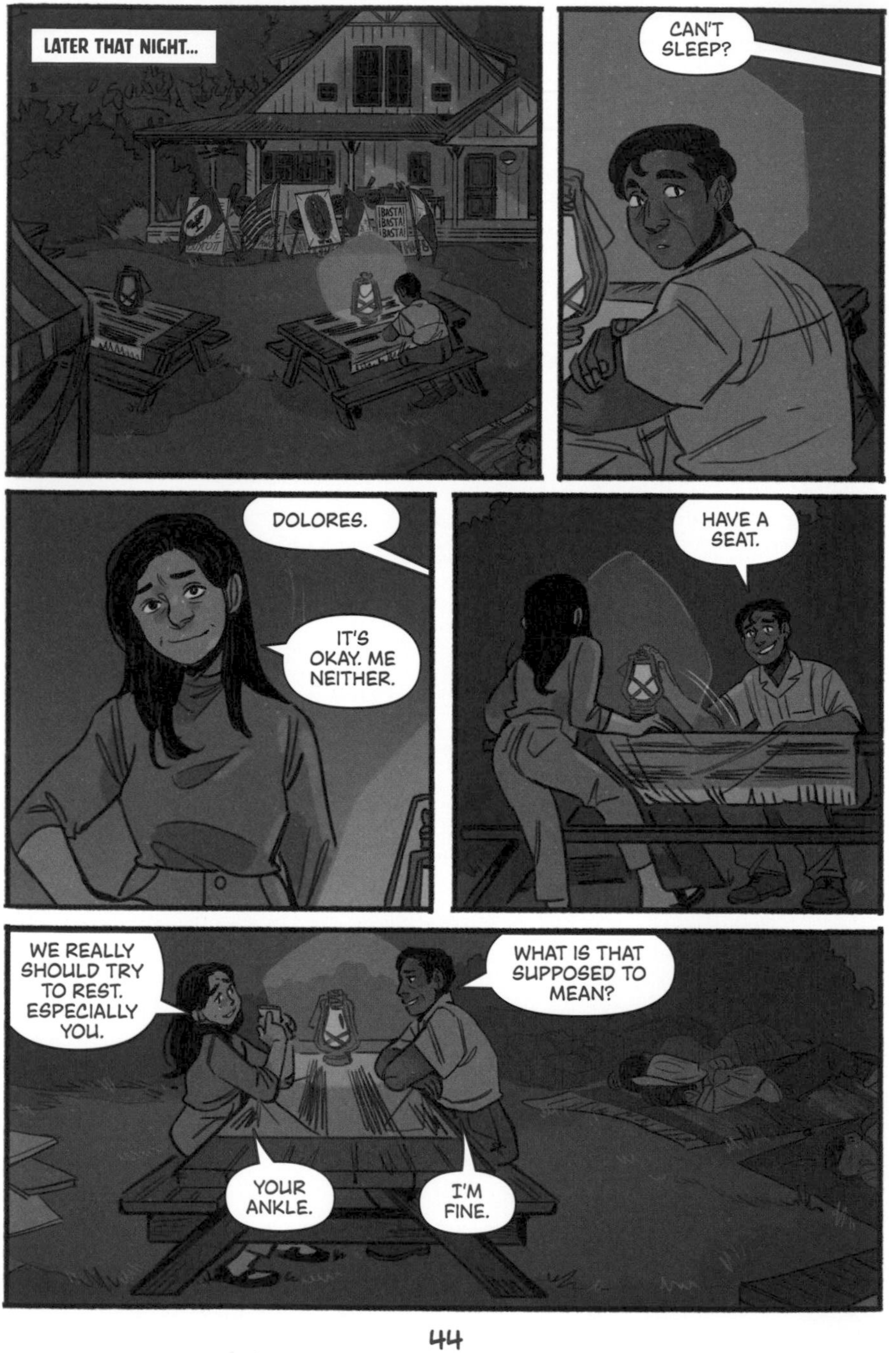
LATER THAT NIGHT...
BASTA! BASTA! BASTA!
CAN'T SLEEP?
DOLORES.
IT'S OKAY. ME NEITHER.
HAVE A SEAT.
WE REALLY SHOULD TRY TO REST. ESPECIALLY YOU.
WHAT IS THAT SUPPOSED TO MEAN?
YOUR ANKLE.
I'M FINE.

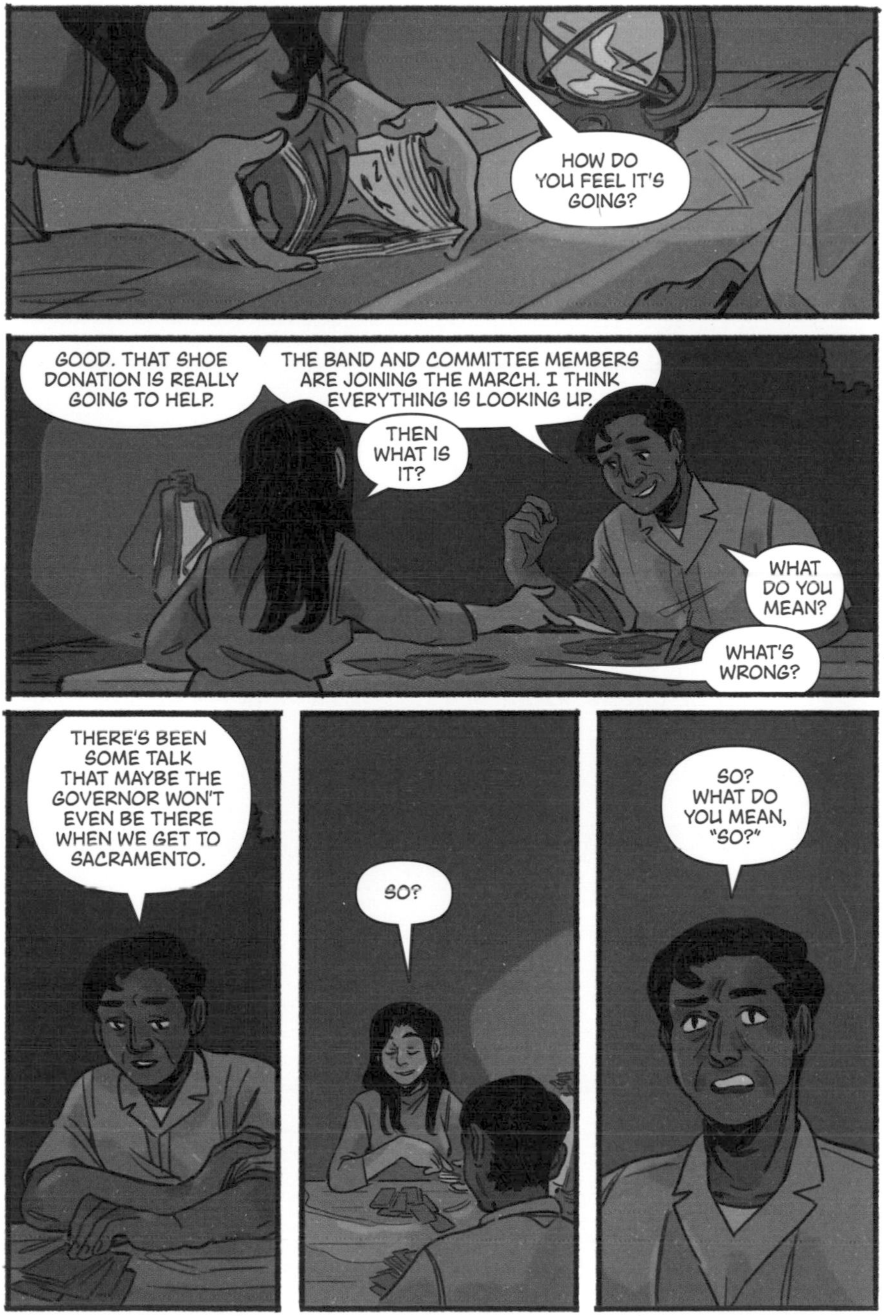
HOW DO YOU FEEL IT'S GOING?
GOOD. THAT SHOE DONATION IS REALLY GOING TO HELP.
THE BAND AND COMMITTEE MEMBERS ARE JOINING THE MARCH. I THINK EVERYTHING IS LOOKING UP.
THEN WHAT IS IT?
WHAT DO YOU MEAN?
WHAT'S WRONG?
THERE'S BEEN SOME TALK THAT MAYBE THE GOVERNOR WON'T EVEN BE THERE WHEN WE GET TO SACRAMENTO.
SO?
SO? WHAT DO YOU MEAN, "SO?"

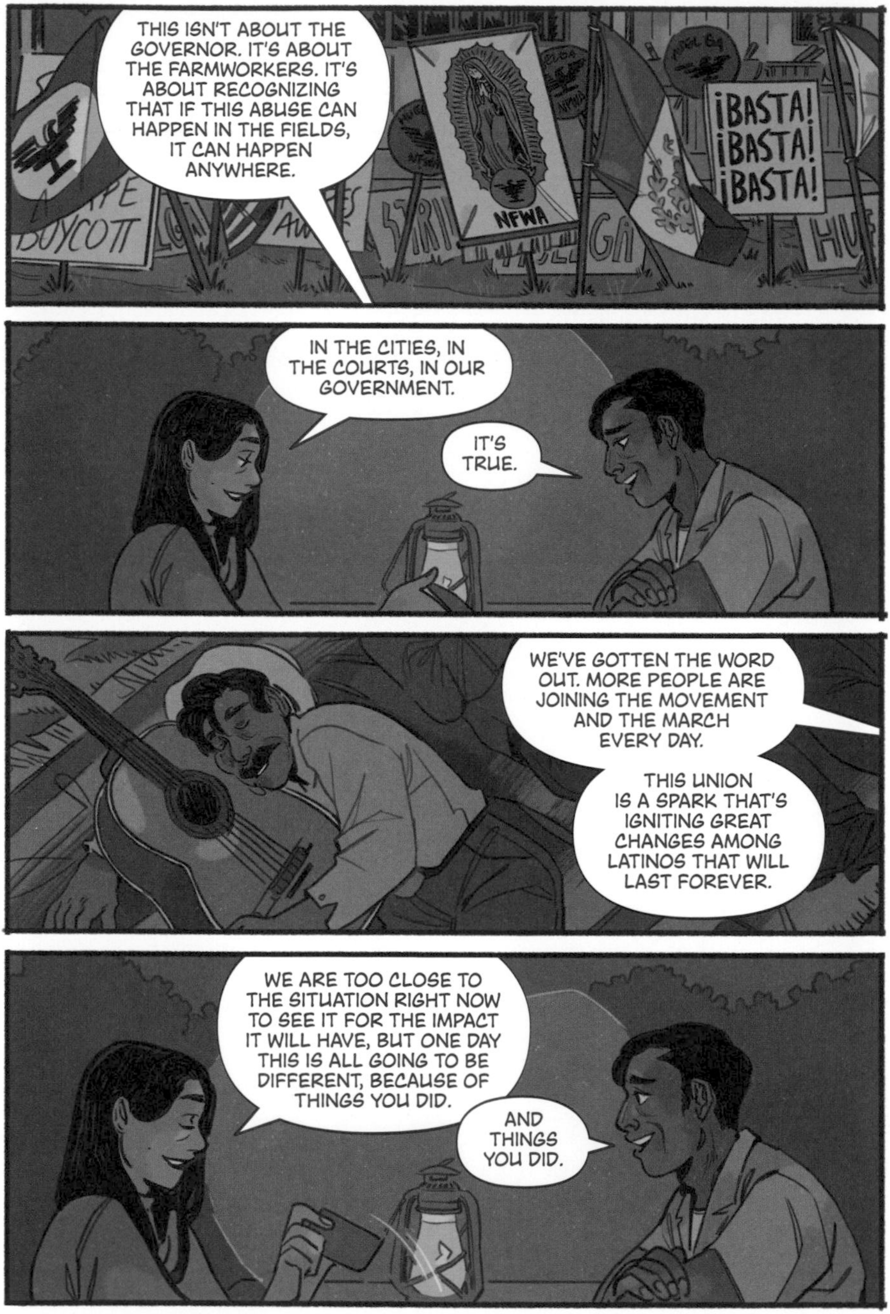
THIS ISN'T ABOUT THE GOVERNOR. IT'S ABOUT THE FARMWORKERS. IT'S ABOUT RECOGNIZING THAT IF THIS ABUSE CAN HAPPEN IN THE FIELDS, IT CAN HAPPEN ANYWHERE.
¡BASTA! ¡BASTA! ¡BASTA!
NFWA
BOYCOTT
IN THE CITIES, IN THE COURTS, IN OUR GOVERNMENT.
IT'S TRUE.
WE'VE GOTTEN THE WORD OUT. MORE PEOPLE ARE JOINING THE MOVEMENT AND THE MARCH EVERY DAY.
THIS UNION IS A SPARK THAT'S IGNITING GREAT CHANGES AMONG LATINOS THAT WILL LAST FOREVER.
WE ARE TOO CLOSE TO THE SITUATION RIGHT NOW TO SEE IT FOR THE IMPACT IT WILL HAVE, BUT ONE DAY THIS IS ALL GOING TO BE DIFFERENT, BECAUSE OF THINGS YOU DID.
AND THINGS YOU DID.

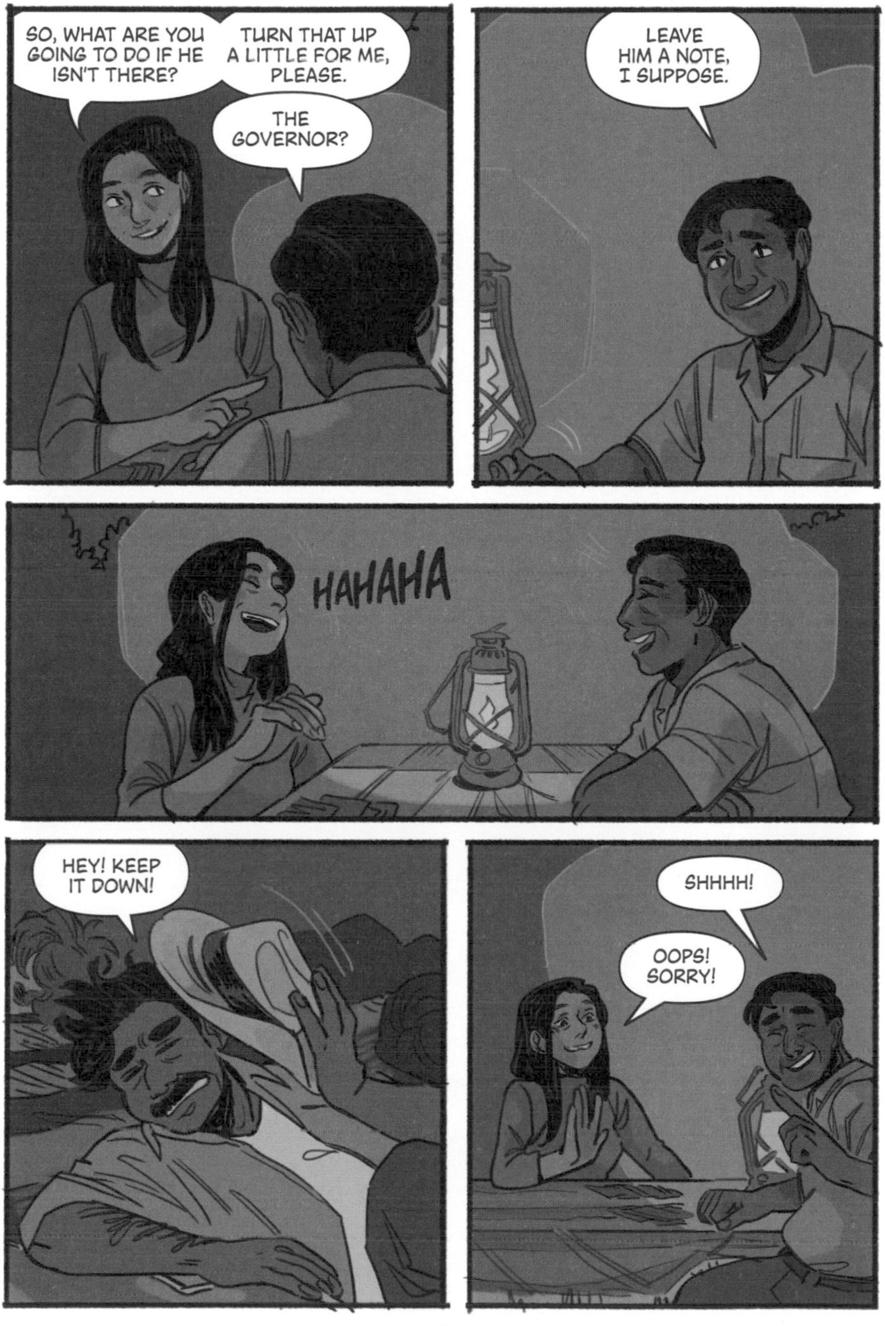
SO, WHAT ARE YOU GOING TO DO IF HE ISN'T THERE?
TURN THAT UP A LITTLE FOR ME, PLEASE.
THE GOVERNOR?
LEAVE HIM A NOTE, I SUPPOSE.
HAHAHA
HEY! KEEP IT DOWN!
SHHHH!
OOPS! SORRY!

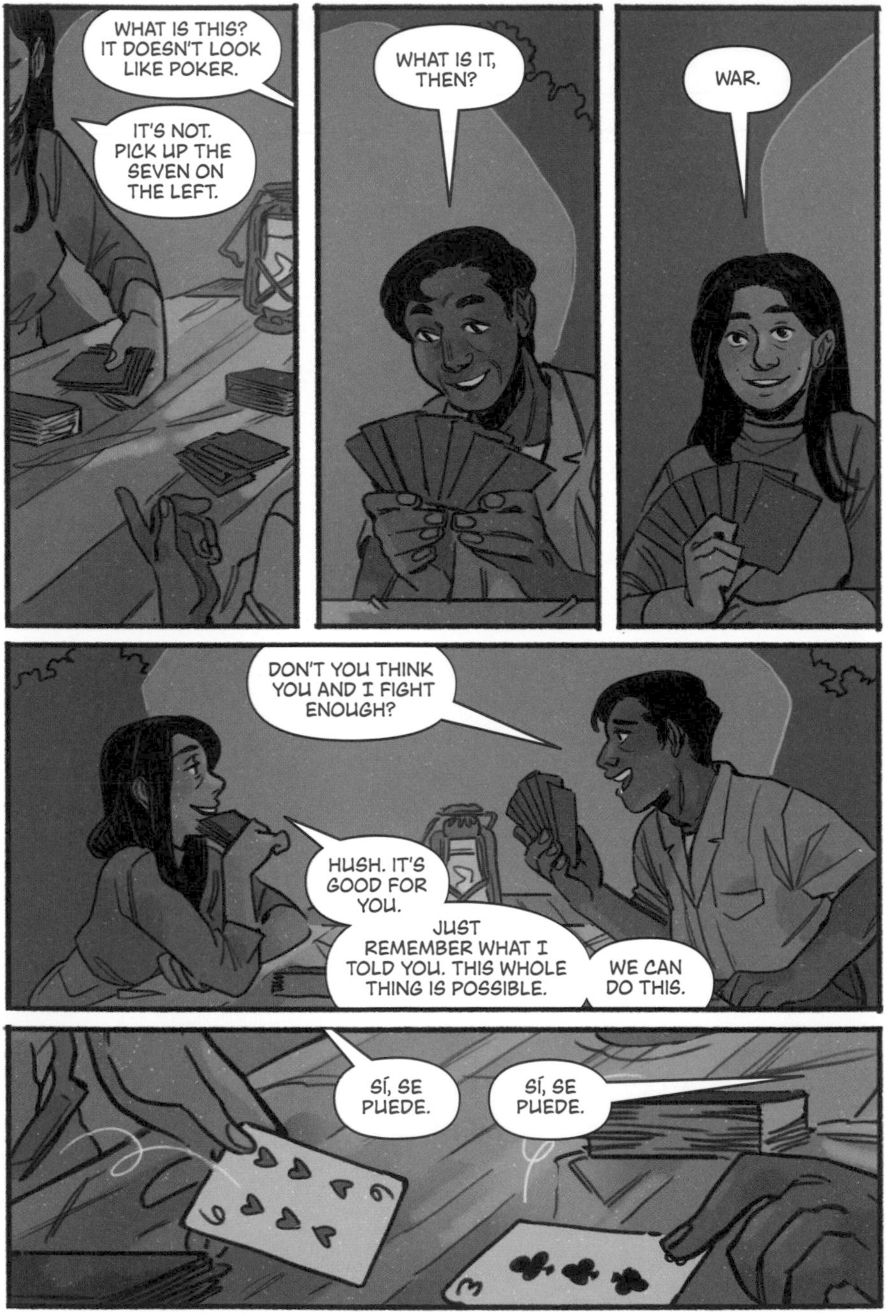
WHAT IS THIS? IT DOESN'T LOOK LIKE POKER.
IT'S NOT. PICK UP THE SEVEN ON THE LEFT.
WHAT IS IT, THEN?
WAR.
DON'T YOU THINK YOU AND I FIGHT ENOUGH?
HUSH. IT'S GOOD FOR YOU.
JUST REMEMBER WHAT I TOLD YOU. THIS WHOLE THING IS POSSIBLE.
WE CAN DO THIS.
SÍ, SE PUEDE.
SÍ, SE PUEDE.

Dolores Huerta

Dolores Clara Fernández was born on April 10, 1930, in Dawson, New Mexico, but spent most of her early childhood in Stockton, California.

Her father, Juan Fernández, was a farmworker, but she was raised mostly by a single mother, Alicia Chavez Fernández, whose community work and independent spirit inspired Dolores to get more involved in activism.

Dolores cofounded the National Farm Workers Association along with Cesar in 1962. Her determination and experience as a member of multiple organizations, including the Girl Scouts, helped her secure government programs like Aid to Families with Dependent Children (AFDC) along with disability protection for farmworkers in California.

In 2008, President Barack Obama adopted a personal quote of Dolores's, "Sí, se puede," which became a popular mantra for his campaign. It means, "Yes, we can," or "Yes, it can be done." In 2012, President Obama awarded Dolores the Presidential Medal of Freedom, the highest award given to a civilian in the United States.

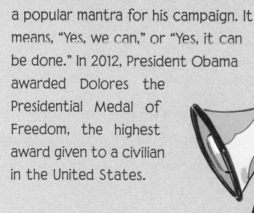

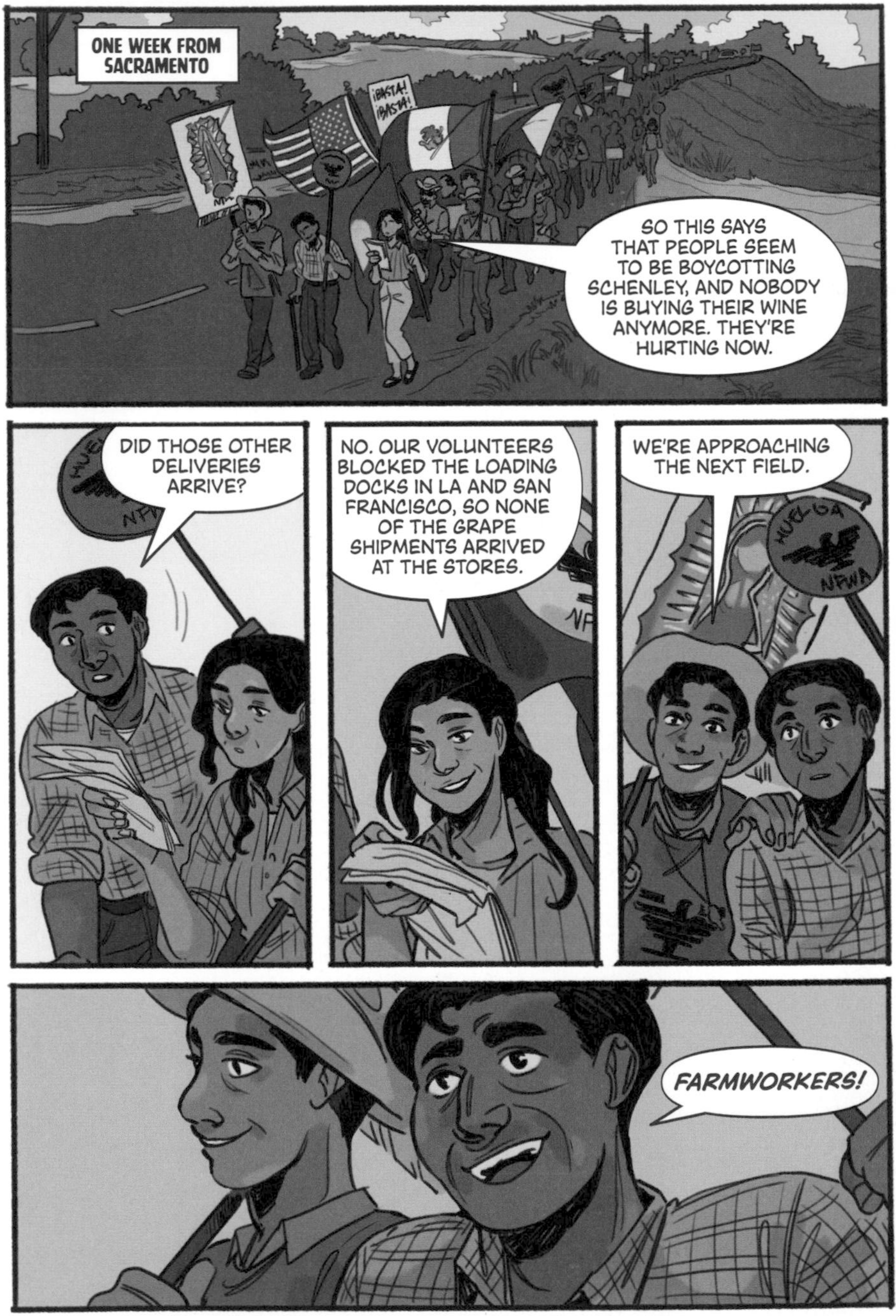
ONE WEEK FROM SACRAMENTO
¡BASTA! ¡BASTA!
SO THIS SAYS THAT PEOPLE SEEM TO BE BOYCOTTING SCHENLEY, AND NOBODY IS BUYING THEIR WINE ANYMORE. THEY'RE HURTING NOW.
DID THOSE OTHER DELIVERIES ARRIVE?
NO. OUR VOLUNTEERS BLOCKED THE LOADING DOCKS IN LA AND SAN FRANCISCO, SO NONE OF THE GRAPE SHIPMENTS ARRIVED AT THE STORES.
WE'RE APPROACHING THE NEXT FIELD.
HUELGA NFWA
FARMWORKERS!

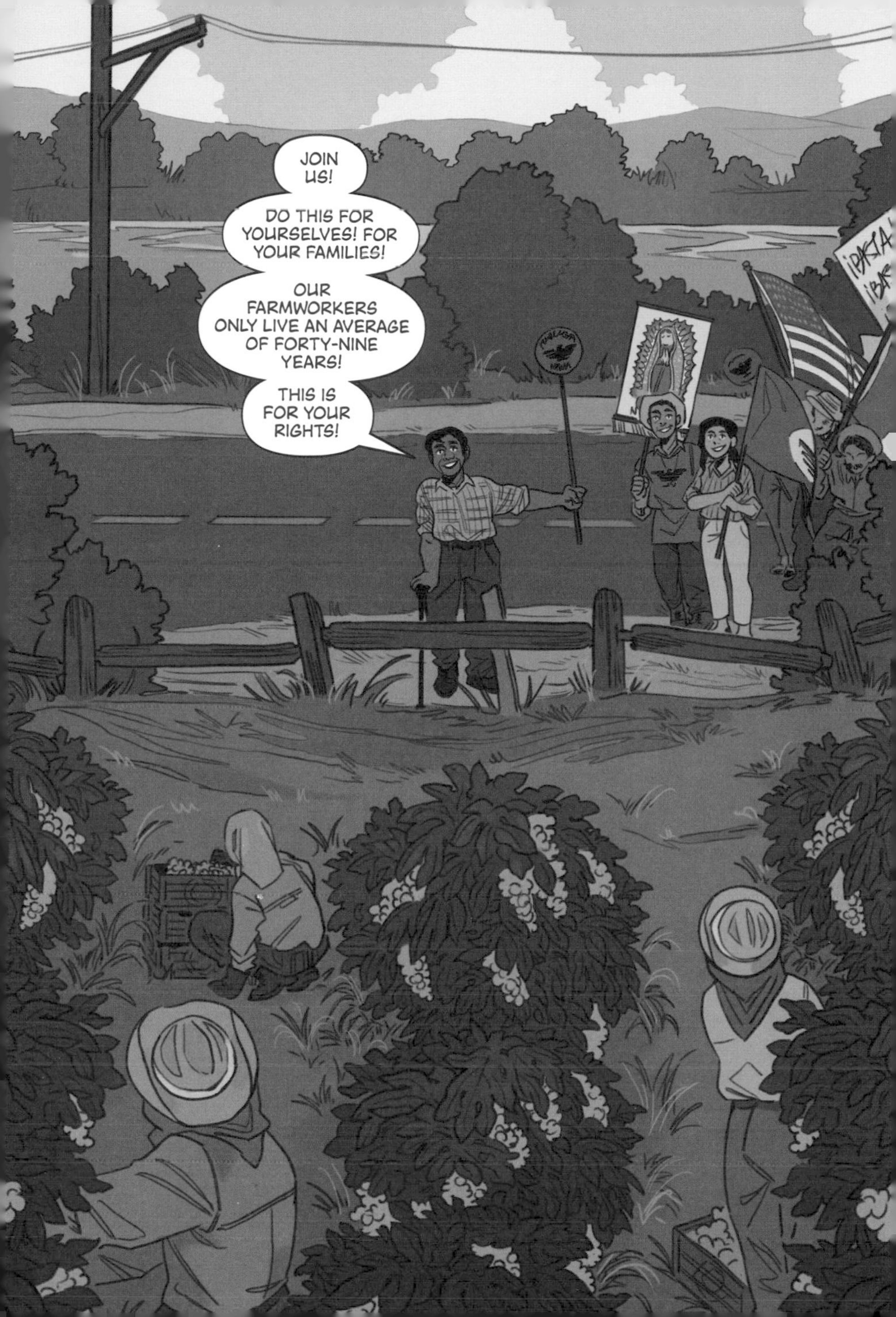
JOIN US!
DO THIS FOR YOURSELVES! FOR YOUR FAMILIES!
OUR FARMWORKERS ONLY LIVE AN AVERAGE OF FORTY-NINE YEARS!
THIS IS FOR YOUR RIGHTS!

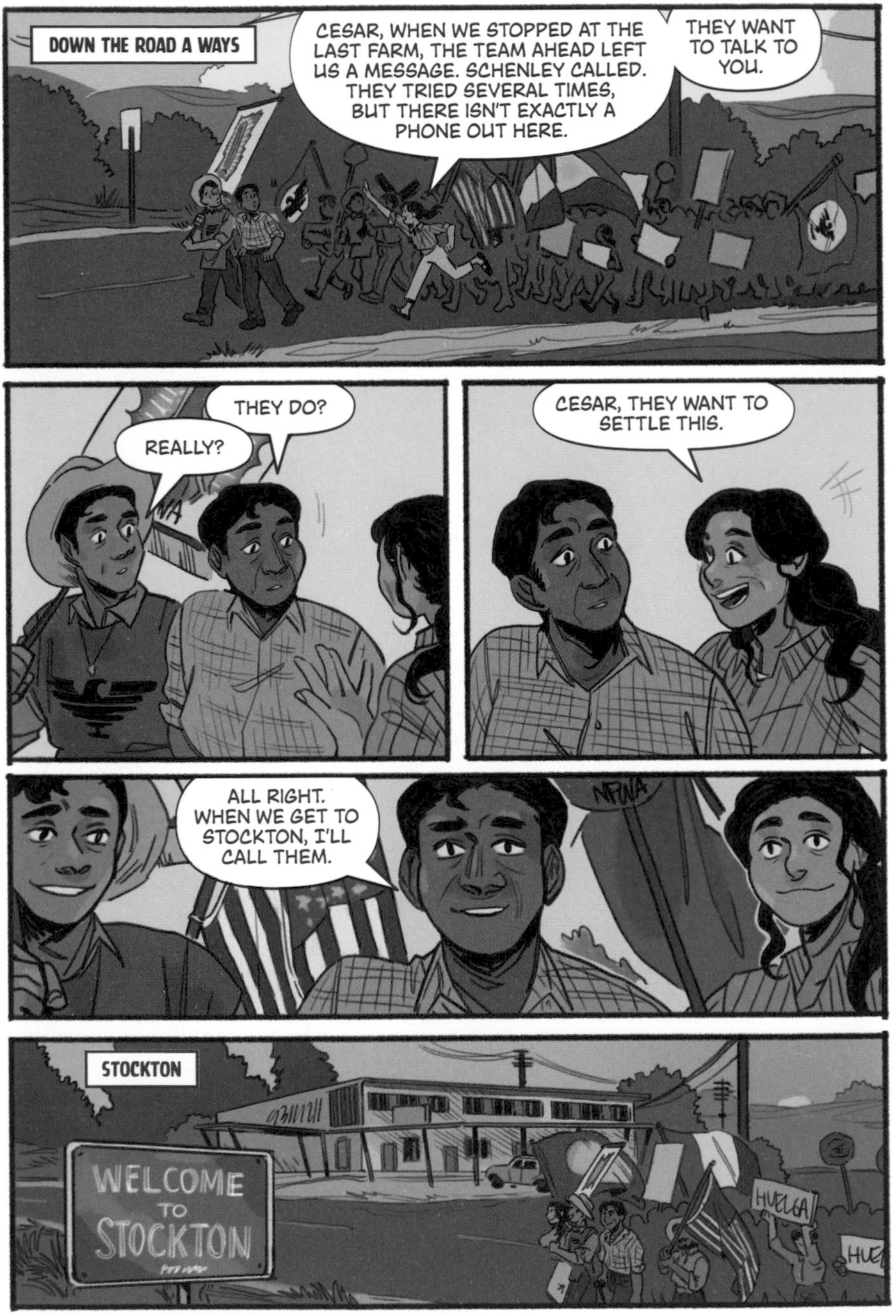
DOWN THE ROAD A WAYS
CESAR, WHEN WE STOPPED AT THE LAST FARM, THE TEAM AHEAD LEFT US A MESSAGE. SCHENLEY CALLED. THEY TRIED SEVERAL TIMES, BUT THERE ISN'T EXACTLY A PHONE OUT HERE.
THEY WANT TO TALK TO YOU.
REALLY?
THEY DO?
CESAR, THEY WANT TO SETTLE THIS.
ALL RIGHT. WHEN WE GET TO STOCKTON, I'LL CALL THEM.
STOCKTON
WELCOME TO STOCKTON
HUELGA

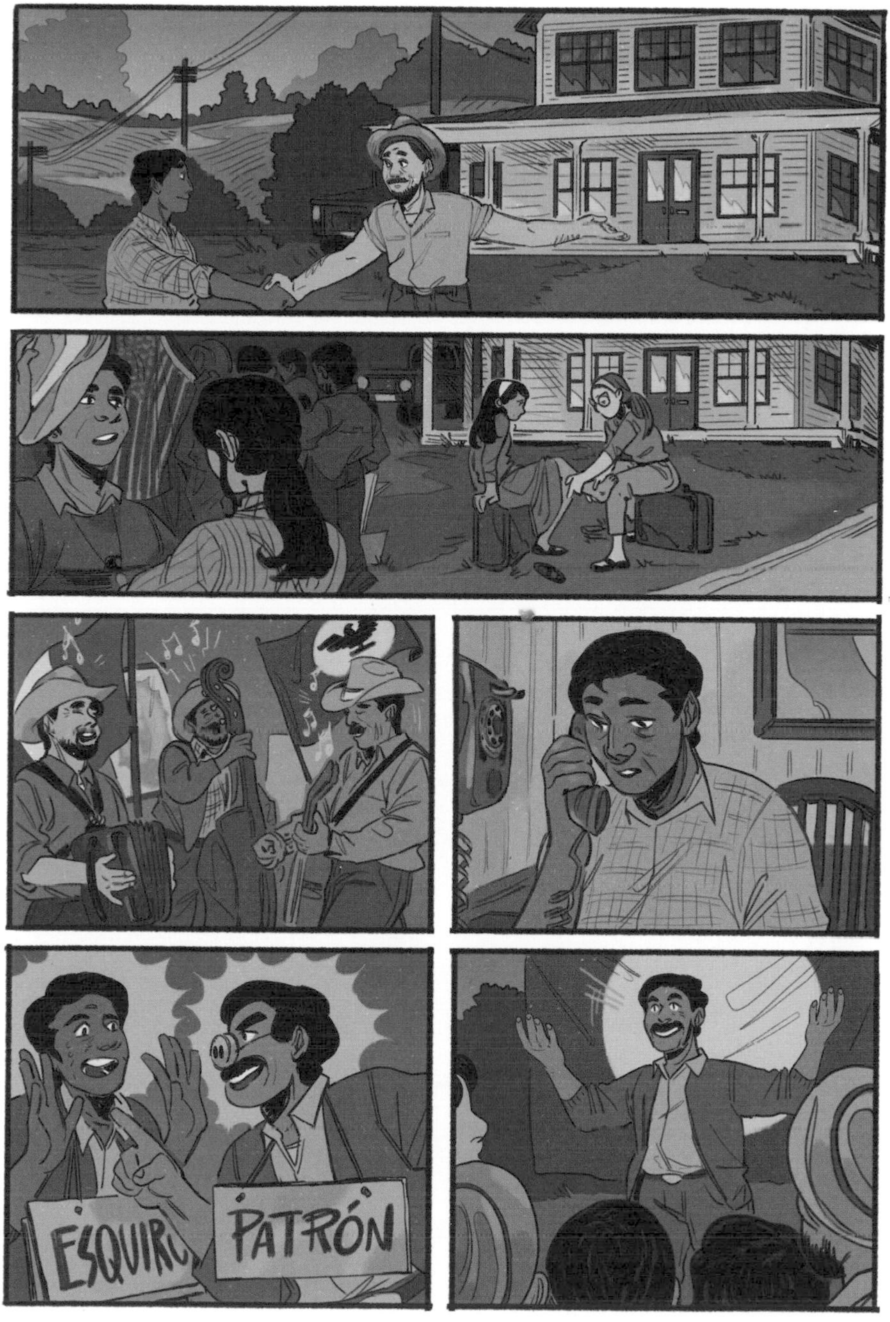
ESQUIR
PATRÓN

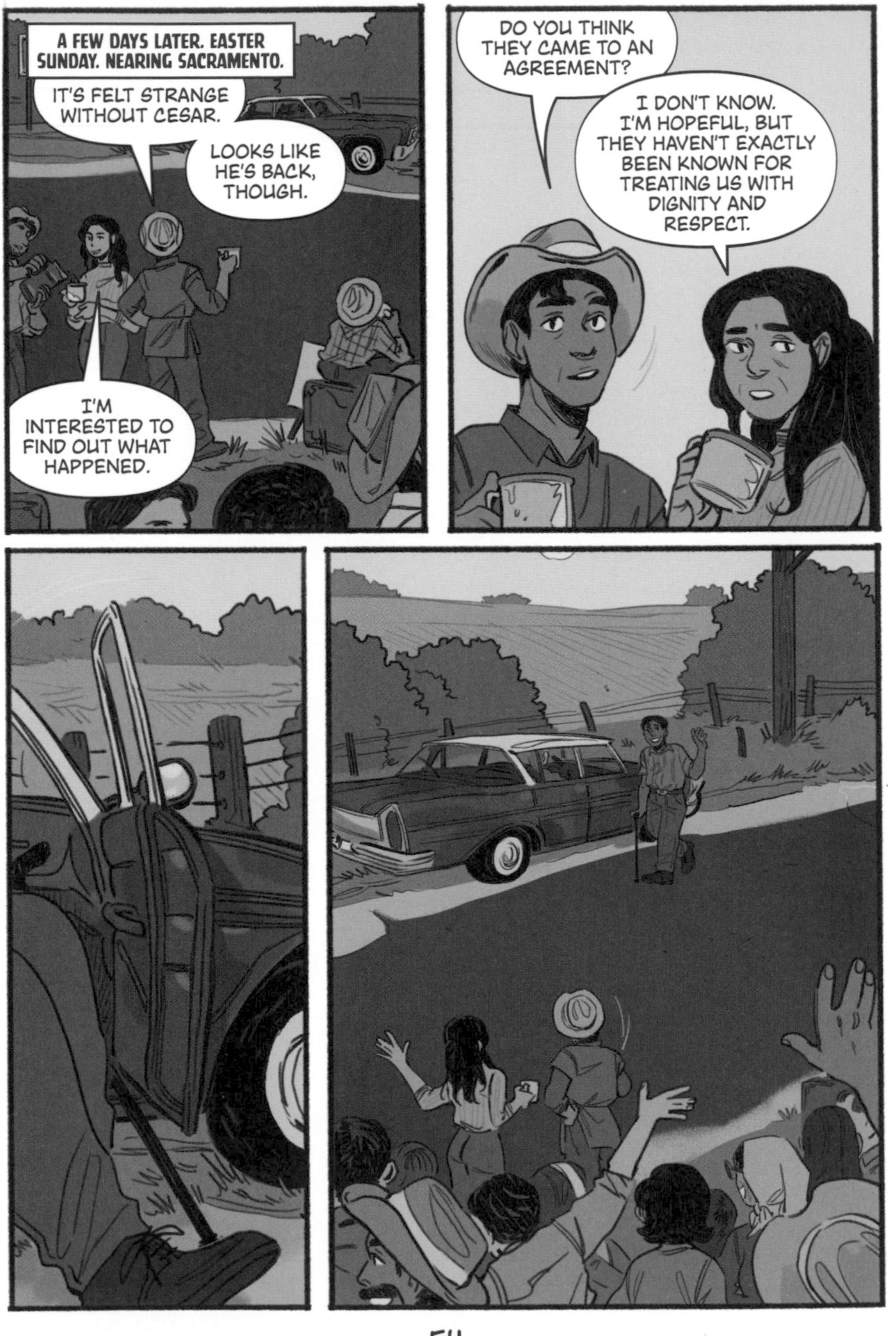
A FEW DAYS LATER. EASTER SUNDAY. NEARING SACRAMENTO.
IT'S FELT STRANGE WITHOUT CESAR.
LOOKS LIKE HE'S BACK, THOUGH.
I'M INTERESTED TO FIND OUT WHAT HAPPENED.
DO YOU THINK THEY CAME TO AN AGREEMENT?
I DON'T KNOW. I'M HOPEFUL, BUT THEY HAVEN'T EXACTLY BEEN KNOWN FOR TREATING US WITH DIGNITY AND RESPECT.

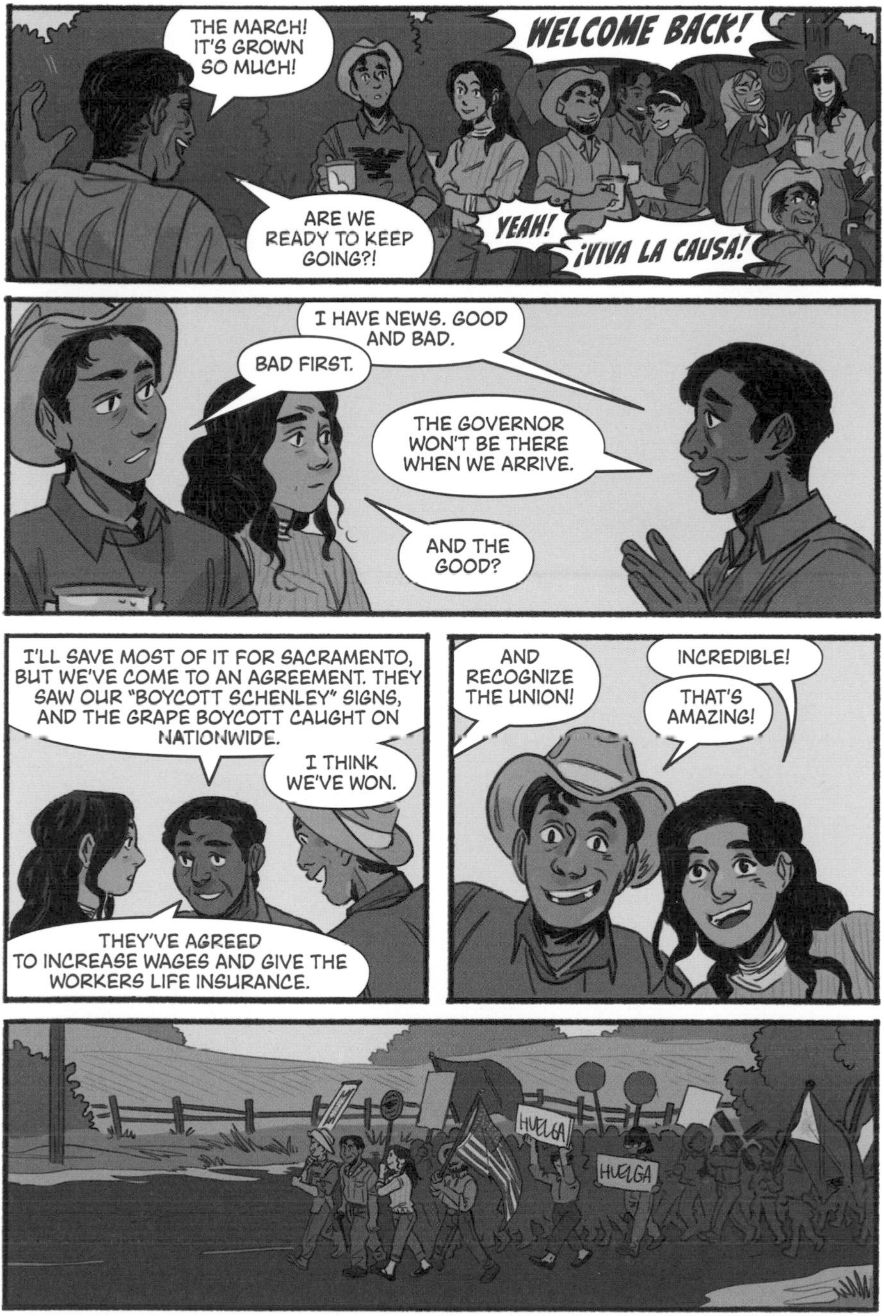
THE MARCH! IT'S GROWN SO MUCH!
WELCOME BACK!
ARE WE READY TO KEEP GOING?!
YEAH!
¡VIVA LA CAUSA!
I HAVE NEWS. GOOD AND BAD.
BAD FIRST.
THE GOVERNOR WON'T BE THERE WHEN WE ARRIVE.
AND THE GOOD?
I'LL SAVE MOST OF IT FOR SACRAMENTO, BUT WE'VE COME TO AN AGREEMENT. THEY SAW OUR "BOYCOTT SCHENLEY" SIGNS, AND THE GRAPE BOYCOTT CAUGHT ON NATIONWIDE.
I THINK WE'VE WON.
THEY'VE AGREED TO INCREASE WAGES AND GIVE THE WORKERS LIFE INSURANCE.
AND RECOGNIZE THE UNION!
INCREDIBLE!
THAT'S AMAZING!
HUELGA
HUELGA

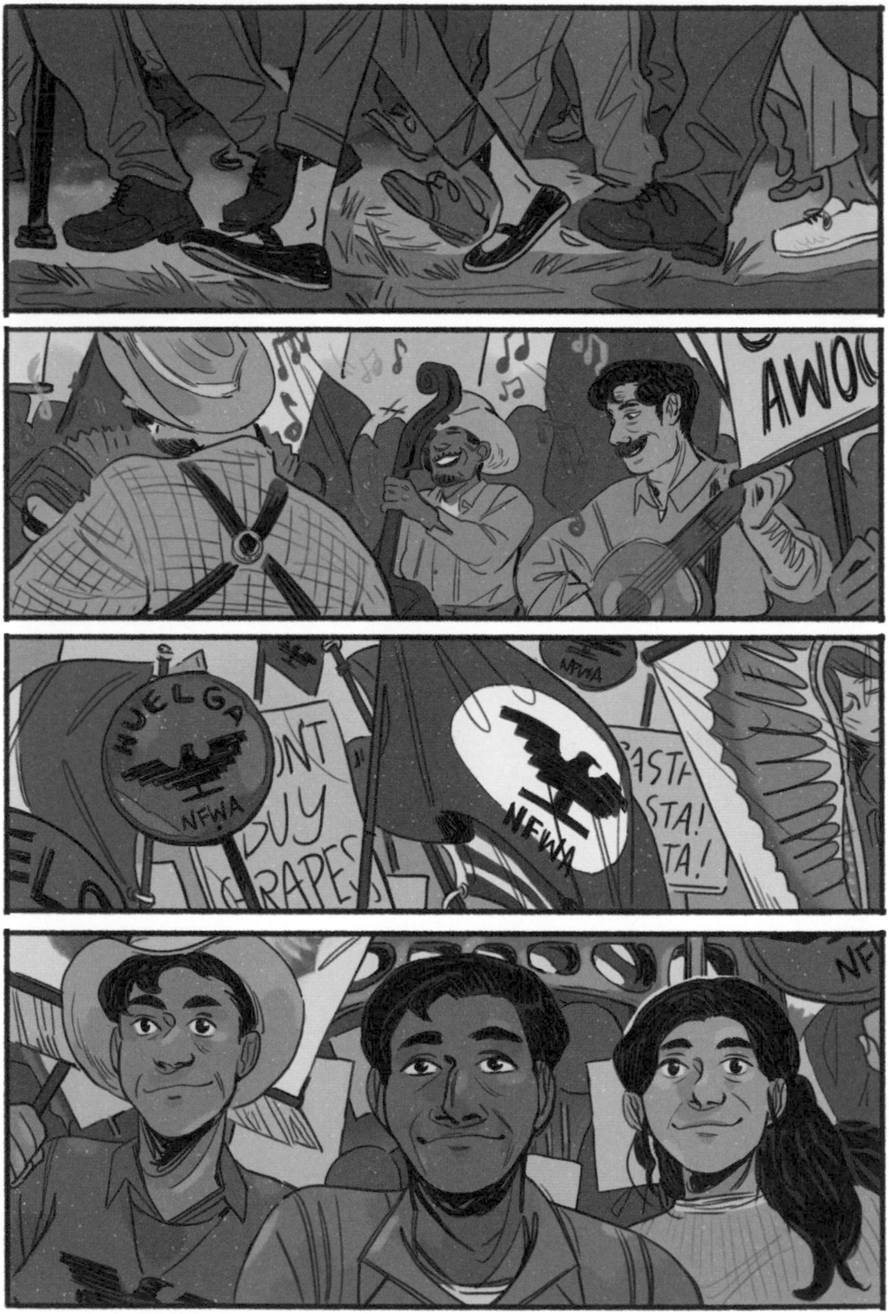
AWOO
HUELGA
NFWA
BUY
NFWA
NFWA

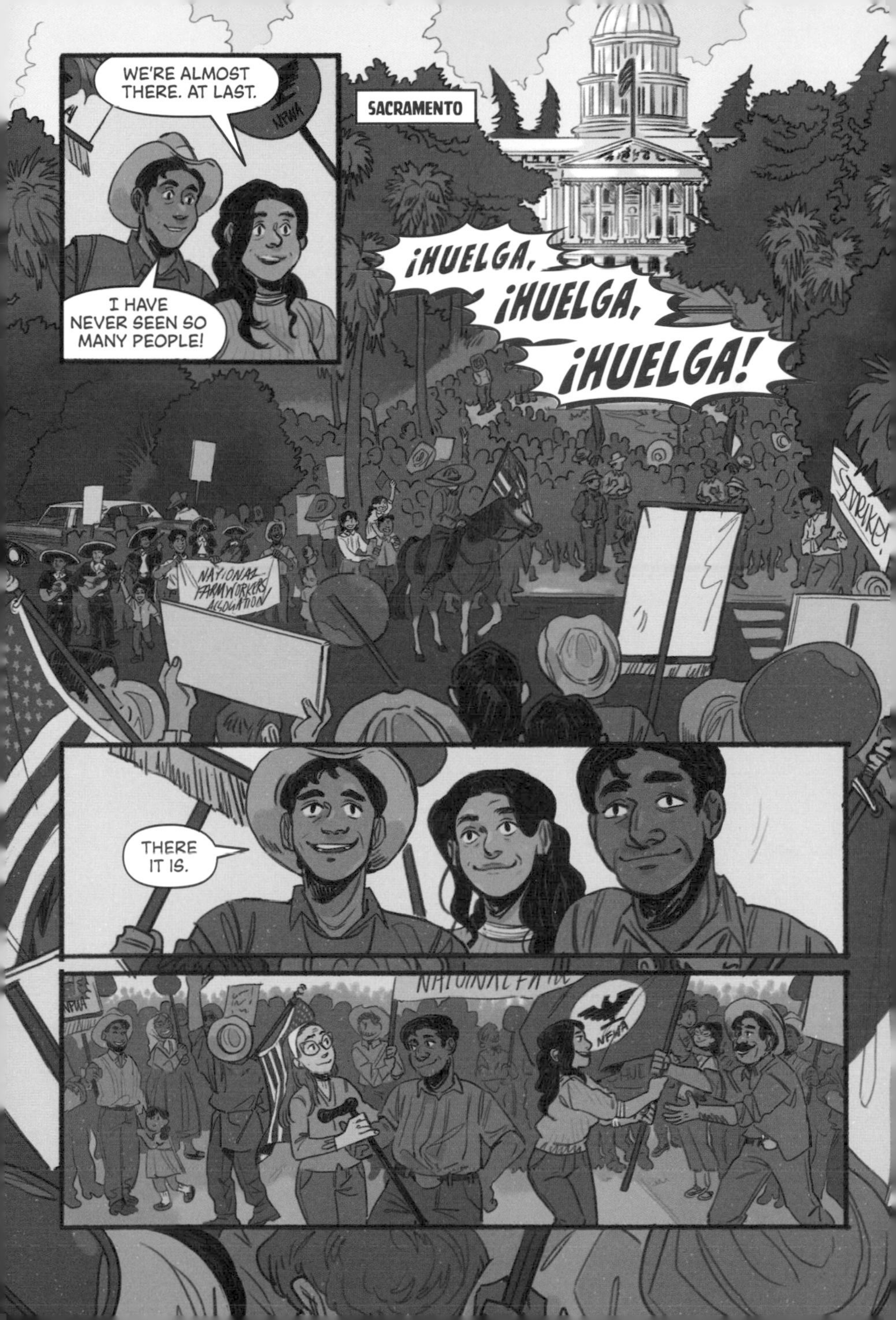
WE'RE ALMOST THERE. AT LAST.
I HAVE NEVER SEEN SO MANY PEOPLE!
SACRAMENTO
¡HUELGA, ¡HUELGA, ¡HUELGA!
NATIONAL FARMWORKERS ASSOCIATION
STRIKE!
THERE IT IS.
NFWA

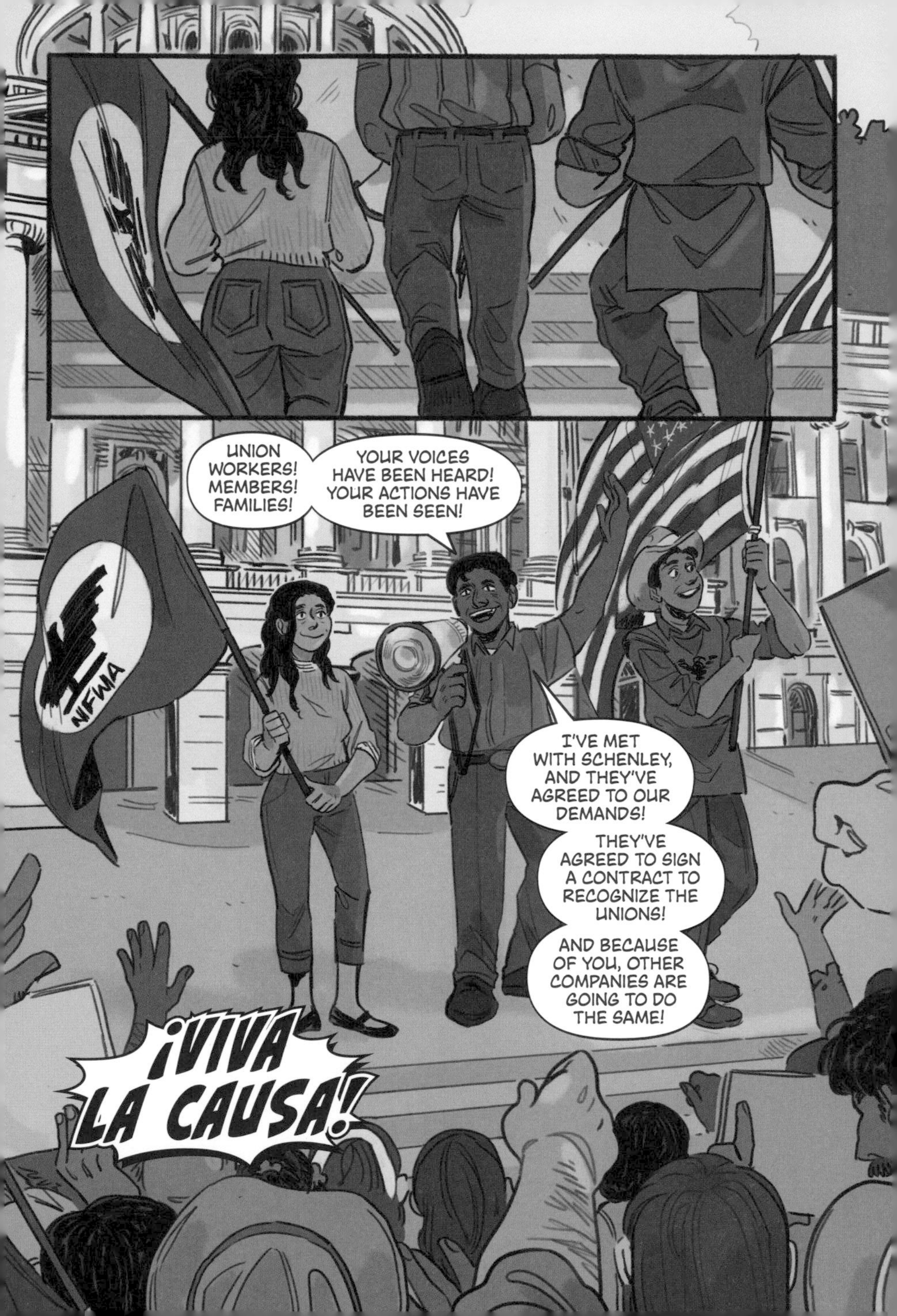
UNION WORKERS! MEMBERS! FAMILIES!
YOUR VOICES HAVE BEEN HEARD! YOUR ACTIONS HAVE BEEN SEEN!
NFWA
I'VE MET WITH SCHENLEY, AND THEY'VE AGREED TO OUR DEMANDS!
THEY'VE AGREED TO SIGN A CONTRACT TO RECOGNIZE THE UNIONS!
AND BECAUSE OF YOU, OTHER COMPANIES ARE GOING TO DO THE SAME!
¡VIVA LA CAUSA!

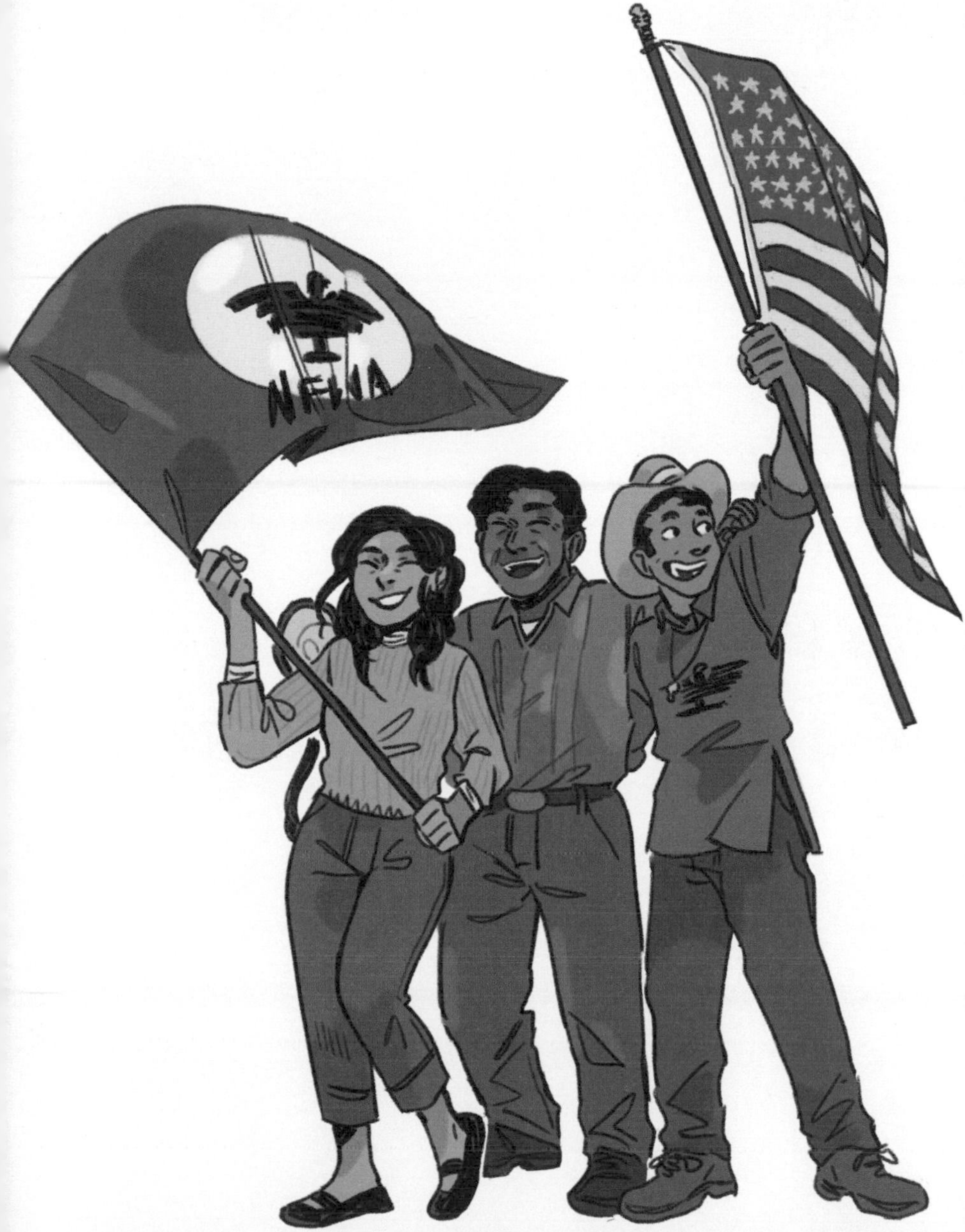
NFWA

Conclusion

In August 1966, the NFWA united with another union, the Agricultural Workers Organizing Committee. The two unions became known as the United Farm Workers. Uniting these two groups made them much stronger, and not long after, Cesar received a telegram from civil rights leader Dr. Martin Luther King Jr. that said, "Our separate struggles are really one—a struggle for freedom, for dignity, and for humanity."

The grape strike went on for over five years. While many agreements were signed, progress was slow. A lot of farmworkers were still left unprotected and grew impatient. In fact, some workers felt that fighting back physically was the only answer. This caused a divide within the union. Cesar, committed to nonviolence, decided to do what Gandhi did: On February 15, 1968, he began a hunger strike to show that violence was not the answer. This meant that he would go without food and only drink water until the violence stopped. The strike was very tough. With every day that passed, he grew weaker. He lost thirty-five pounds! Cesar's wife, Helen Chavez, was worried for his life. Doctors begged him to stop. But the union members heard Cesar's message: All talk of violence stopped from then on, and after twenty-five days, he ended the strike.

In 1969, Cesar expanded his boycott of the grapes into Canada.

He asked stores to stop buying grapes grown in California. By 1970, the farm owners were losing so much money that they agreed to strike a deal with the UFW: They signed contracts that recognized the union and agreed to better working conditions for the farmworkers.

In April 1993, Cesar Chavez passed away at the age of sixty-six. The impact that Cesar had on farmworkers, migrant workers, and people of all kinds is recognized around the world today. After his death, he was awarded the Presidential Medal of Freedom by President Bill Clinton and the Águila Azteca (the Aztec Eagle), the highest award given to foreign citizens by the Mexican government.

Timeline of Cesar Chavez's Life

1927 — Cesar Estrada Chavez is born on March 31 near Yuma, Arizona

1938 — Cesar's family leaves Arizona and moves to California to begin work as migrant farmworkers

1948 — Marries Helen Fabela on October 22

1955 — Meets Dolores Huerta

1962 — Cesar and Dolores form the National Farm Workers Association

— The NFWA flag is revealed at the first meeting for the National Farm Workers Association

1965 — Agrees to join the strike against the grape growers in the San Joaquin Valley

1966 — Leads a 340-mile march from Delano to California's capitol building in Sacramento in March and April

1968 — Fasts for twenty-five days in protest against violent farmworker actions

1970 — Grape growers sign contracts on July 29, ending the five-year grape strike

1988 — Fasts for thirty-six days in protest against pesticide use

1993 — Dies in San Luis, Arizona, on April 23

Bibliography

*Books for young readers

Bratt, Peter, dir. *Dolores.* 5 Stick Films, 2017.

Brunner, Borgna. "Timeline: Cesar Chavez." February 28, 2017.
Infoplease.com. https://www.infoplease.com/history/hispanic-heritage/timeline-cesar-chavez.

"Cesar Chavez and the Farmworker Movement." May 29, 2014.
University of California Television, YouTube video, 51:35.
https://www.youtube.com/watch?v=-2_3mWGl5ws&t=672s.

Fuentes, Ed. "How One Flag Went From Representing Farmworkers to Flying for the Entire Latino Community." April 2, 2014. **TakePart. com.** http://www.takepart.com/article/2014/04/02/cultural-history-ufw-flag/.

García, Mario T. *The Gospel of César Chávez: My Faith in Action* Lanham, MD: Sheed & Ward, 2007.

*Rau, Dana Meachen. *Who Was Cesar Chavez?* New York: Penguin Workshop, 2017.

Valdez, Louis. "Commentary of Luis Valdez: The Plan of Delano."
Farmworker Movement Documentation Project: Presented by the UC San Diego Library. https://libraries.ucsd.edu/farmworkermovement/essays/essays/Plan%20of%20Delano.pdf.

ABOUT THE CREATORS

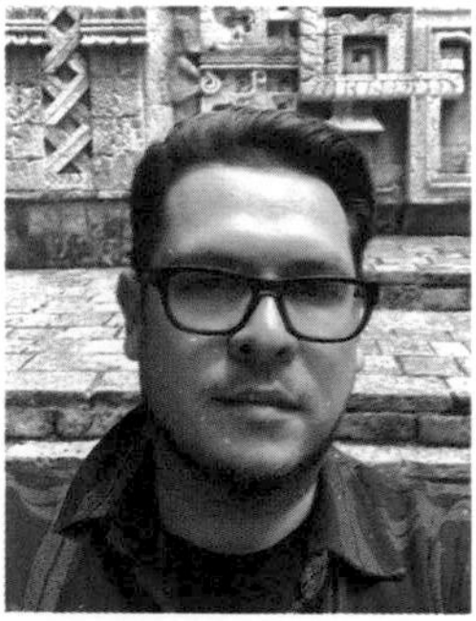

Terry Blas is an illustrator and writer based in Portland, Oregon. His auto-bio comics *You Say Latino* and *You Say LatinX* were featured on NPR, OPB, Vox.com, and Cosmo.com. Terry's work has appeared in the comics The Amazing World of Gumball, Adventure Time, and Steven Universe. His first graphic novel, *Dead Weight: Murder at Camp Bloom*, was named by YALSA as a 2019 Quick Pick for Reluctant Young Readers. His second graphic novel, *Hotel Dare*, is an all-ages, fantasy epic inspired by his childhood in Mexico. His third book, *Lifetime Passes*, will be published by Surely Books.

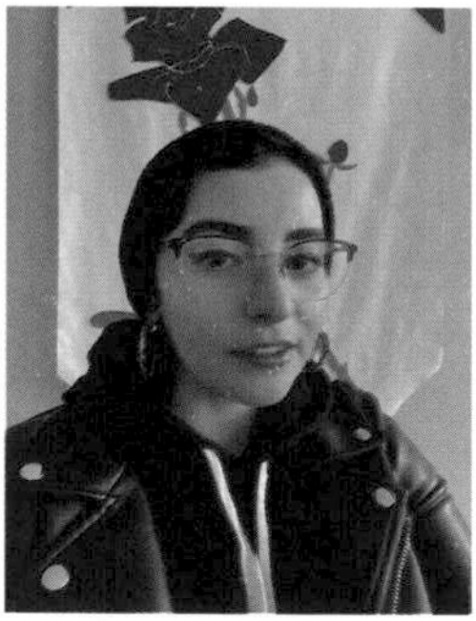

Mar Julia is an Ignatz Award-nominated cartoonist and illustrator living in Baltimore, Maryland. Their debut graphic novel, *Brownstone*, a collaboration with writer Samuel Teer, is scheduled for release from Versify in 2022.